THE ULTIMATE THUNDERBIRD 2024 MAIL APP GUIDE FOR BEGINNERS

WIENIUS FAWIENSON

Copyright © 2024 Wienius Fawienson
All rights reserved.

INTRODUCTION

In the digital age, where communication drives personal connections and powers businesses, email remains at the heart of all our interactions. We may navigate a whirlwind of apps and social media platforms, but for structured, professional, and long-lasting communication, email continues to stand out. Despite the rise of chat and instant messaging, email's unique advantages—its formality, reliability, and versatility—keep it indispensable. However, managing emails efficiently requires more than just reading and replying to messages; it demands a dedicated tool that organizes, streamlines, and elevates your entire email experience. Mozilla Thunderbird, an open-source email client, is one such tool that is perfectly equipped to transform how you handle email.

Email clients today face the challenge of offering simplicity and ease for new users while also providing depth and customization options for advanced users. Thunderbird strikes this delicate balance, making it a top choice among professionals, students, and personal users alike. As a powerful yet user-friendly application, Thunderbird allows users to handle multiple email accounts, organize communications seamlessly, and customize their experience to fit their unique preferences. For those new to Thunderbird, the interface and myriad features may seem daunting at first, but with this guide, you'll soon find that Thunderbird can be a trusted ally in managing your email effortlessly.

Thunderbird has earned its reputation as a reliable, safe, and flexible email client. Unlike proprietary software, Thunderbird is built on a foundation of transparency and user empowerment. Being an open-source project by Mozilla, it benefits from a dedicated community of developers, security experts, and contributors who continuously enhance its features and address user concerns. This sense of community-driven development ensures Thunderbird evolves alongside its users' needs, consistently adapting to new trends, technologies, and security practices. When you choose Thunderbird, you're not only choosing a robust email client but also joining a network of individuals committed to a free and open internet.

For beginners, the journey into the world of email management with Thunderbird starts with understanding the essentials: installation, setup, and the core tools that make Thunderbird unique. The process of setting up Thunderbird is straightforward, with helpful prompts and guidance, yet still offers opportunities for advanced users to tailor the setup to their preferences. This adaptability means Thunderbird grows with you—whether you're just starting to use it for personal emails or managing multiple business accounts, calendars, and custom filters for efficiency.

Beyond the basic setup, Thunderbird offers rich personalization options that allow you to make the email client truly yours. From customizing themes and layouts to setting up keyboard shortcuts, Thunderbird empowers you to optimize your workspace, improving both the look and functionality to match your style and workflow. As you grow more comfortable with the app, you'll discover features designed to simplify and streamline email management. Thunderbird allows users to categorize, filter, and search for emails in powerful ways, making the search for that important message or document quick and painless. If you've ever found yourself overwhelmed by an inbox cluttered with unread messages, you'll find Thunderbird's management tools a welcome solution.

In addition to email management, Thunderbird includes an address book feature that simplifies organizing and retrieving contact information. This is especially useful if you manage a large number of contacts across different fields or if your work requires regular outreach. The address book integrates seamlessly with your emails and calendar, so you can quickly pull up relevant information or set up reminders for meetings and follow-ups. Thunderbird's ability to centralize these tools within one application helps you avoid the frustration of switching between programs, boosting productivity and ensuring you stay on top of your communications.

Thunderbird's calendar and task management tools are invaluable for those who prefer an all-in-one workspace. No longer just an email client, Thunderbird enables you to plan your days, set goals, and organize meetings without ever leaving the app. These tools enhance the overall experience by giving you a comprehensive view of your day at a glance, coordinating emails, events, and tasks all in one place. The seamless integration of these features minimizes the need for external calendar applications, which is a boon for users seeking simplicity and coherence in their digital lives.

As you become more proficient with Thunderbird, you'll encounter its advanced features, which are designed for users who need more than just a standard email client. Thunderbird supports add-ons and extensions, allowing you to expand its functionality according to your needs. Whether you need specific tools for productivity, additional layers of security, or customization options, Thunderbird's community-developed add-ons offer solutions tailored to almost every scenario. For instance, users in industries where email security is paramount can leverage Thunderbird's encryption features to protect sensitive communications. Furthermore, Thunderbird's compatibility with various email protocols and its ability to handle multiple accounts securely and efficiently make it an indispensable tool for those who manage complex email needs.

Security is a central pillar of Thunderbird's development philosophy. Email remains one of the most commonly exploited digital communication methods, with phishing, spam, and malware attacks constantly evolving to target unsuspecting users. Thunderbird takes these threats seriously, equipping the app with built-in tools and features to shield your data from unauthorized access. From robust spam filtering to end-to-end encryption options, Thunderbird is committed to safeguarding your privacy. You'll learn how to make the most of these security features, allowing you to communicate confidently, knowing your information remains protected.

However, even the best software can sometimes present challenges. Fortunately, Thunderbird is backed by extensive resources, documentation, and a dedicated support community to help you troubleshoot and overcome any issues you may encounter. From simple connection problems to more complex configuration adjustments, you'll find solutions to common issues that arise, allowing you to maintain an uninterrupted workflow. Thunderbird's active community forums are a valuable asset, with users and developers ready to share insights and advice. Whether you're facing a minor hiccup or a major technical concern, these resources make it easy to resolve issues quickly.

For users ready to dive deeper, Thunderbird offers advanced settings and scripting capabilities, giving you the power to automate tasks, set up custom workflows, and enhance your productivity even further. Scripting allows Thunderbird to be more than just an email client—it becomes a personalized assistant capable of automating repetitive tasks and freeing up your time for more important work. Imagine setting up automatic responses, sorting emails based on specific criteria, or triggering actions based on the content of a message. With Thunderbird's scripting options, you can transform the way you work, achieving efficiency that goes beyond traditional email management.

By the time you complete this journey with Thunderbird, you'll possess more than just a working knowledge of the app; you'll have a toolkit of strategies and skills for effective digital communication. You'll gain a deeper understanding of email best practices, security principles, and productivity hacks that extend beyond Thunderbird itself. Thunderbird can become a foundational part of your digital life, helping you not only manage your emails but also organize your contacts, calendars, and tasks with precision and ease.

This guide will walk you step-by-step through Thunderbird's many capabilities, guiding you from the basics to the advanced features that can elevate your productivity. Whether you are setting up Thunderbird for the first time or looking to refine your skills, you'll find insights, tips, and strategies designed to help you get the most out of this powerful tool. Each section builds on the last, giving you a comprehensive understanding of how to leverage Thunderbird's full potential.

Embracing Thunderbird as your primary email client is not just about switching software; it's about rethinking the way you manage communication. With its comprehensive features and user-centered design, Thunderbird stands as a versatile platform that adapts to your evolving needs. As you begin this journey, take each step with curiosity and openness. Thunderbird is not merely a tool but an empowering solution that makes email management a rewarding experience. By exploring Thunderbird's functionality and mastering its nuances, you're embarking on a path toward greater control, efficiency, and confidence in managing your digital world.

Let this guide be your companion, illuminating the path to a streamlined, secure, and fully personalized email experience. As you progress through each section, you'll develop the skills to harness Thunderbird's full capabilities, transforming the way you interact with email. By the end of this book, Thunderbird will be more than just another program on your computer; it will be an indispensable asset in your digital toolkit. Welcome to a new era of email management—one where you're in control, empowered, and ready to make the most of every message, meeting, and opportunity that comes your way.

CONTENTS

INTRODUCTION iii

CONTENTS ix

Chapter 1: Introducing to Thunderbird Mail 1

Chapter 2: Installation and Initial Setup 29

Chapter 3: Personalization and Customization Options 35

Chapter 4: Managing Your Emails Effectively 43

Chapter 5: Organizing Contacts and Address Book 49

Chapter 6: Using Calendar and Task Management 56

Chapter 7: Exploring Advanced Features 69

Chapter 8: Ensuring Email Security and Encryption 92

Chapter 9: Troubleshooting and Support Tips 101

Chapter 10: Mastering Advanced Settings 110

Chapter 11: Creating and Using Scripts 121

CONCLUSION 125

CHAPTER 1: INTRODUCING TO THUNDERBIRD MAIL

I. WHAT IS THUNDERBIRD?

Overview of Thunderbird as an Email and Productivity Tool

Mozilla Thunderbird, commonly referred to as Thunderbird, is a powerful, open-source email client developed by the Mozilla Foundation—the same organization responsible for the popular Firefox web browser. Launched in 2003, Thunderbird has since evolved into one of the most trusted and versatile email platforms available today, especially among users seeking a free alternative to paid email applications. Its design prioritizes privacy, customization, and flexibility, making it a favored choice for both personal and professional email management.

At its core, Thunderbird allows users to manage multiple email accounts from a single platform, whether they are personal accounts, work emails, or a mix of both. It supports major email protocols like POP3, IMAP, and SMTP, enabling it to connect with nearly any email provider. This compatibility makes Thunderbird a particularly appealing choice for users who need an email client that can adapt to a variety of services without compromising functionality. But Thunderbird isn't just an email client; it's a robust productivity tool, complete with features that go beyond sending and receiving messages. From task management to a customizable interface, Thunderbird offers a rich suite of tools designed to boost organization, streamline communication, and simplify the user's digital workflow.

Key Features of Thunderbird

Thunderbird's core features make it a competitive choice for users seeking a secure, customizable, and efficient email management solution. Here's a look at some of the highlights:

1. **Multiple Account Management**

   Thunderbird enables seamless integration of multiple email accounts. Whether you have a Gmail account, an Outlook address, or a business email from a custom domain, Thunderbird lets you manage them all under one roof. This flexibility is particularly useful for users who juggle various accounts daily, as it eliminates the need to log in and out of different accounts or access different websites to check emails.

2. **Intuitive User Interface**

   Designed with ease of use in mind, Thunderbird's interface is clean, modern, and easy to navigate. It offers a familiar, folder-based structure that allows users to categorize emails by folders or tags, a layout similar to popular webmail services but with added flexibility. Users can also customize the interface by rearranging sections or using add-ons to introduce new functionalities, making it adaptable to individual preferences.

3. **Robust Security and Privacy Features**

   Mozilla is known for its commitment to user privacy, and Thunderbird reflects this philosophy. With features like end-to-end encryption, built-in spam filtering, and options for blocking remote content, Thunderbird keeps users' emails secure. Users can also enable two-factor authentication for added security and have control over the amount of data they share. Thunderbird's open-source nature adds an additional layer of trust, as the code is open to scrutiny, and any potential vulnerabilities are quickly addressed by the community.

4. **Calendar and Task Management**

   Thunderbird includes the "Lightning" calendar add-on, which lets users schedule appointments, create tasks, and set reminders—all within the same application. For individuals and professionals who rely on a streamlined workflow, having a built-in calendar and task manager can reduce the need to switch between multiple apps or devices to keep track of schedules.

5. **Customizability Through Add-Ons**

   One of Thunderbird's standout features is its ability to be customized with add-ons and extensions. Similar to how Firefox allows extensions to enhance the browsing experience, Thunderbird's add-ons extend its functionality. From aesthetics to productivity-boosting features, users can install various add-ons to tailor Thunderbird precisely to their needs. Examples include add-ons for enhanced address book management, email templates, themes, and even third-party integrations.

6. **Advanced Email Management Tools**

   Thunderbird's email management tools go beyond basic functions. With features like message filters, search capabilities, and customizable sorting options, users can organize their inboxes to reduce clutter and improve efficiency. The email filtering feature, for instance, allows users to create rules for organizing messages automatically based on sender, subject, keywords, and more. Additionally, Thunderbird's powerful search function enables users to find specific emails quickly, even if they have thousands of messages stored.

Thunderbird as a Productivity Tool

In today's fast-paced world, managing multiple communications, schedules, and tasks effectively is essential, and Thunderbird rises to the occasion by providing features that support enhanced productivity.

1. **Unified Inbox**

   A unified inbox brings all incoming emails into a single view, which can save users significant time. Instead of checking each inbox separately, users can see all new messages in one location. This feature is particularly helpful for those managing multiple roles, clients, or projects, as it provides a comprehensive overview of all incoming communication.

2. **Offline Access**

   Thunderbird allows users to access their emails and other information offline, making it a useful tool for people who may not always have a reliable internet connection. This is particularly valuable for professionals who need to prepare responses, review emails, or update their schedules while on the go.

3. **Integrated Chat Feature**

   Thunderbird also supports various chat protocols, allowing users to communicate in real-time with contacts through services like Google Talk, XMPP, and IRC. For teams that prefer real-time discussions or for users who want to centralize their communication channels, this built-in chat function can be a helpful productivity tool.

4. **Email Archiving**

   Archiving helps users manage their inboxes by moving old or inactive messages out of the main inbox but keeping them easily accessible for reference. This function is particularly useful for professionals who need to keep records for compliance or project documentation purposes, as it offers a way to retain important emails without cluttering active folders.

5. **Personalized Workflows and Automation**

   Thunderbird's filters and automation capabilities allow users to set up personalized workflows that can automatically sort, tag, or even forward emails based on specific conditions. By establishing these automated rules, users can manage their inboxes more efficiently and focus on higher-priority tasks, which is invaluable in a busy professional setting.

Why Choose Thunderbird?

Beyond its feature set, Thunderbird's open-source status means it has an active community of developers and users who contribute to its improvement and security. This transparency is a major draw for those who prioritize digital privacy. Additionally, Thunderbird's flexibility and versatility make it suitable for a wide range of users, from students organizing study materials to professionals handling complex business communications.

With no subscription fees or hidden costs, Thunderbird provides a robust email and productivity solution accessible to everyone. It's especially popular among users who value control over their digital tools and seek a high level of customization. Thunderbird combines core email functionalities with powerful organizational tools, security, and flexibility, making it a comprehensive productivity tool that can cater to both beginner and advanced users. For anyone looking to optimize their email experience and streamline digital workflows, Thunderbird is a reliable and powerful choice.

II. THE DEVELOPMENT HISTORY OF THUNDERBIRD

Evolution and Key Milestones in Thunderbird's Journey

The history of Mozilla Thunderbird is a testament to the importance of open-source software and the dedication of a global community to building an effective, privacy-focused, and user-driven email client. Developed by the Mozilla Foundation, Thunderbird has carved a unique place among email applications, largely because of its focus on privacy, extensibility, and customization. From its initial release in 2003 to its latest 2024 version, Thunderbird has evolved significantly, adapting to the ever-changing digital landscape and continuing to meet the needs of users around the world.

Early Beginnings: The Rise of an Open-Source Email Client

The roots of Thunderbird can be traced back to the early 2000s, a period when email was rapidly becoming an essential tool for personal and professional communication. The Mozilla Foundation, which had recently launched the Firefox web browser, recognized a need for an equally robust and secure open-source email client. Thus, Thunderbird was conceived as a counterpart to Firefox, aimed at providing users with a free, secure, and customizable email application.

In July 2003, Thunderbird made its debut as an open-source project, with the first official release (Thunderbird 0.1) arriving in July of that year. Like many open-source projects, Thunderbird's development was collaborative, relying on contributions from a global community of developers, designers, and users. The Mozilla Foundation's mission—to create open-source software that respected user privacy and freedom—became the guiding principle for Thunderbird's development, and it quickly gained popularity among tech enthusiasts and privacy-conscious users.

Key Milestones in Thunderbird's Evolution

1. **Thunderbird 1.0 (2004): The First Major Release** The first full release of Thunderbird, version 1.0, launched in December 2004, marking a milestone for Mozilla and the open-source community. This version introduced a range of essential features that would become standard for email clients, including spam filtering, support for multiple accounts, and customizable folder management. Thunderbird 1.0 also featured tabbed email browsing and a clean, user-friendly interface. This was a major accomplishment for the Mozilla team and established Thunderbird as a strong competitor to proprietary email clients like Microsoft Outlook and Apple Mail.

2. **The Expansion of Features (2005-2010)** Over the next several years, Thunderbird's feature set continued to grow. By 2005, the Mozilla Foundation had officially launched Thunderbird 1.5, which introduced message filtering, an advanced search function, and improved security protocols like phishing protection. During this time, the concept of add-ons and extensions also took shape, allowing users to further customize Thunderbird with themes and additional functionality.

In 2006, Mozilla decided to split Thunderbird's development from Firefox to allow each project to develop independently. This decision eventually led to the creation of Mozilla Messaging, a subsidiary tasked solely with developing Thunderbird. With a focused team, Thunderbird saw continued improvements, including better integration with third-party services, improved spam filtering, and advanced email sorting and searching capabilities.

3. **Mozilla Messaging and the Shift to Community Development (2011)** In 2011, Mozilla Messaging merged back into the Mozilla Foundation, and Mozilla made the decision to halt direct development of new Thunderbird features. Instead, Mozilla chose to place Thunderbird into a mode of "extended support," focusing on maintaining stability and security while relying on the open-source community for new feature development. This move worried some users, but the Thunderbird community remained active, and contributions from dedicated developers ensured the software continued to evolve.

4. **Thunderbird 3.0 (2009) and the Introduction of Major Productivity Tools** Released in 2009, Thunderbird 3.0 was a significant update that introduced tabbed email viewing, allowing users to open multiple emails in separate tabs, similar to how one would browse multiple tabs in Firefox. This release also included better search features, message archiving options, and a new address book design. The improvements made Thunderbird more competitive, allowing it to appeal to users who required robust productivity tools integrated into their email client.

5. **The Thunderbird Council (2014): A New Era of Community-Led Development** With Mozilla's reduced involvement, a group of dedicated Thunderbird developers and community members formed the Thunderbird Council in 2014. The Council was responsible for coordinating development, managing releases, and making strategic decisions about the project's future. This transition marked the beginning of Thunderbird as a truly community-driven project, guided by the values of open-source collaboration and user-centric design.

6. **Thunderbird 52 (2017): Modernization and Feature Refinement** The release of Thunderbird 52 in 2017 was a notable milestone, as it brought a range of updates that improved compatibility with modern operating systems and email protocols. Key features included OAuth2 support for Gmail, enabling secure and simplified login, along with enhancements to the calendar function, integrated chat, and improved performance. By this point, Thunderbird was becoming increasingly popular not only among individual users but also among small businesses and organizations looking for a reliable email solution.

7. **Thunderbird 68 and the Integration with OpenPGP (2019)** Thunderbird 68, released in 2019, marked a major step forward in email security with the

integration of OpenPGP encryption. This allowed users to easily encrypt and decrypt messages, enhancing email privacy—a core principle of the Thunderbird project. Alongside these security improvements, Thunderbird 68 also featured a redesigned interface, compatibility improvements, and a more streamlined approach to add-ons, helping Thunderbird to stay relevant in a landscape with constantly evolving digital security requirements.

8. **Thunderbird 78 and Modern Security Protocols (2020)** Thunderbird 78, launched in 2020, introduced a new look with an updated UI and further improvements in security, making it easier for users to manage OpenPGP encryption and adopt the latest security practices. This version also included Dark Mode, increased add-on compatibility, and other usability enhancements that helped modernize the software.

9. **Thunderbird 91 and the Path Toward the 2024 Version** With the release of Thunderbird 91 in 2021, Thunderbird became increasingly streamlined and feature-rich, preparing the way for the major 2024 update. Thunderbird 91 focused on integration, allowing for better syncing across devices, enhanced address book functionality, and task management improvements. At this stage, Thunderbird was cementing itself as a tool for not only email but also productivity management.

Looking Ahead: The Future of Thunderbird in 2024 and Beyond

As Thunderbird approaches its latest iteration in 2024, the project is committed to staying relevant by incorporating modern design principles, supporting the latest email standards, and enhancing security features. Under the guidance of the Thunderbird Council and an active developer community, the roadmap for Thunderbird includes deeper integration with cloud services, increased compatibility with mobile devices, and continued focus on customization and flexibility.

The ongoing success of Thunderbird showcases the power of open-source software and the enduring impact of a project that prioritizes user privacy and choice. From its humble beginnings as an open-source alternative to major email clients, Thunderbird has grown into a fully featured, versatile, and highly respected productivity tool used by millions worldwide. As technology evolves, Thunderbird is poised to continue adapting and meeting the needs of users, driven by its strong community and unwavering commitment to open-source principles.

III. WHY CHOOSE THUNDERBIRD?

Benefits and Unique Features of Using Thunderbird

Mozilla Thunderbird stands out as a powerful and versatile email client in a market dominated by proprietary options like Microsoft Outlook and Gmail. As a free, open-source tool with extensive customization options, Thunderbird attracts users who value privacy, flexibility, and control over their email experience. Designed by the Mozilla Foundation—the organization behind the Firefox browser—Thunderbird emphasizes security, ease of use, and adaptability, offering a range of features that cater to both personal and professional users. Here's an in-depth look at the benefits and unique features that make Thunderbird a compelling choice.

1. Open-Source and Free to Use

One of the most appealing aspects of Thunderbird is its open-source nature. Unlike many email clients that require monthly subscriptions or license fees, Thunderbird is entirely free. It has a robust community of developers who contribute to its evolution, ensuring that users benefit from continuous improvements and security updates without any cost. The open-source model means Thunderbird's code is open for scrutiny, which fosters transparency and trust. Users don't have to worry about hidden fees or advertising embedded in the software—a common concern with many free email platforms.

2. Privacy and Security

Thunderbird was developed by Mozilla, an organization known for prioritizing user privacy and security. Unlike many email services that track user data for targeted advertising, Thunderbird doesn't monitor or monetize user activity. It includes features like built-in spam filters, protection against phishing attempts, and options to block remote content in emails, which keeps users safe from potentially malicious content.

For those who prioritize email security, Thunderbird also offers OpenPGP encryption for end-to-end encrypted messaging. This feature enables users to send encrypted emails, ensuring that only the intended recipient can read the message. It's a rare feature in the email client world, making Thunderbird particularly appealing for privacy-conscious individuals, journalists, and organizations handling sensitive information.

3. Multi-Account Management

Thunderbird's ability to manage multiple email accounts from one interface is another reason it stands out. The client supports major email protocols like IMAP, POP3, and SMTP, enabling users to configure accounts from nearly any email provider, whether they're using Gmail, Outlook, Yahoo, or a custom business domain.

Thunderbird's multi-account management goes beyond just inbox access; it offers a unified inbox view that consolidates all incoming messages, allowing users to view and manage their emails from different accounts in one place. This is particularly helpful for professionals who juggle multiple roles, clients, or projects and need quick access to all their communications without logging in and out of different accounts or switching between platforms.

4. Customization and Add-Ons

One of Thunderbird's defining features is its customizability. Users can personalize the layout, add new features, and even alter the appearance of Thunderbird with themes and extensions. Thunderbird offers an extensive library of add-ons developed by both Mozilla and third-party developers, similar to Firefox's add-ons ecosystem.

For example, users can download add-ons that help with organizing contacts, managing tasks, or scheduling emails. Themes allow users to change the look and feel of Thunderbird to suit their preferences, whether they prefer a minimalist interface or something more visually detailed. This flexibility in customization makes Thunderbird a highly adaptable tool that can be modified to fit the needs of each user, which is rare among other email clients.

5. Advanced Email Management

Efficient email management is essential for staying organized and productive, and Thunderbird's tools for organizing and managing emails are impressive. It includes robust message filtering and tagging features, allowing users to automatically sort incoming emails based on criteria like sender, keywords, or subject line. Users can set up custom tags for categorizing emails by project, priority, or type, making it easier to find important messages at a glance.

Additionally, Thunderbird offers a powerful search function that allows users to locate emails quickly, even in large, complex inboxes. The search bar supports advanced search filters, helping users find specific emails based on sender, date, or other criteria. For people who deal with hundreds or thousands of messages daily, these management tools are invaluable.

6. Integrated Calendar and Task Management

Thunderbird's calendar feature, powered by the "Lightning" add-on, allows users to manage appointments, schedule events, and create tasks—all within the same application. Unlike many email clients that require external software for calendar functionality, Thunderbird's integrated calendar is streamlined and fully customizable, helping users stay on top of schedules without switching applications.

Task management within Thunderbird enables users to set reminders, assign due dates, and track progress on projects. This functionality makes Thunderbird a true productivity tool, allowing users to organize not only their emails but also their tasks and calendars in a single, cohesive platform. For small business owners, freelancers, or project managers, this can be a significant asset.

7. Offline Access

Unlike web-based email clients that require an internet connection to access emails, Thunderbird allows users to download their emails for offline use. This is particularly useful for people who frequently travel or have limited internet access. Offline access allows users to read, compose, and organize their emails without a live connection, which can then be synchronized once they are back online. For professionals working in remote areas or frequent travelers, this feature offers convenience and reliability.

8. Cross-Platform Compatibility

Thunderbird is compatible with Windows, macOS, and Linux, making it a versatile choice for users across different operating systems. Whether you're on a PC at work, a MacBook at home, or a Linux machine in a development environment, Thunderbird provides a consistent experience. Its open-source nature also means that it's easy for developers to maintain compatibility with these systems, even as operating systems are updated over time.

9. Organized Address Book and Contact Management

Thunderbird's built-in address book enables users to store, organize, and search their contacts with ease. It offers a straightforward way to manage contacts and even includes fields for detailed information, such as phone numbers, addresses, and notes. For users who frequently email a large number of contacts, the address book's ability to group contacts and create mailing lists is particularly helpful.

Thunderbird also supports LDAP (Lightweight Directory Access Protocol), which allows it to integrate with corporate directories. This feature is beneficial for businesses or organizations where team members need access to shared contact information, making it easier to communicate within a network or organization.

10. Community Support and Continuous Development

Thunderbird's development is supported by a global community of contributors, which means that new features, security patches, and bug fixes are released regularly. The Thunderbird Council, a group of developers and community members, coordinates this development to keep the software relevant and secure. Users can provide feedback, report issues, or even contribute to Thunderbird's codebase, creating a feedback loop that keeps Thunderbird evolving in response to user needs.

Additionally, because Thunderbird is open-source, its development isn't tied to corporate interests. Unlike proprietary email platforms, Thunderbird is not driven by advertising or user data monetization, which helps keep its development aligned with the interests of its users rather than corporate stakeholders.

Final Thoughts: Why Thunderbird?

Thunderbird offers a powerful combination of security, flexibility, and efficiency. Its open-source nature, coupled with its extensive feature set and community-driven development, makes it ideal for users who want more control over their email and productivity tools. By focusing on privacy, advanced email management, and seamless customization, Thunderbird sets itself apart from conventional email clients, providing a solution that appeals to tech-savvy individuals, privacy advocates, and anyone looking to optimize their communication experience without sacrificing control or security.

With these unique features and benefits, Thunderbird remains a top choice for users seeking a reliable, free, and highly customizable email client that adapts to the needs of both individuals and businesses. Whether you're managing multiple email accounts, organizing a busy calendar, or prioritizing secure communication, Thunderbird provides the tools and features to make it an excellent choice for email management and beyond.

IV. SETTING THE RIGHT MINDSET FOR LEARNING

Approaching Thunderbird with a Productive Mindset

When learning a new software application, especially one as versatile as Mozilla Thunderbird, the approach you take is often as crucial as the technical skills you acquire. Thunderbird is a powerful email client with a host of features aimed at productivity, customization, and security. Yet, to unlock its full potential, adopting a positive and productive mindset is essential. Here's a guide to setting the right mindset for learning Thunderbird effectively, one that fosters exploration, patience, and intentionality in learning.

1. Understanding Your Purpose and Goals

Before diving into Thunderbird, it's helpful to understand *why* you're learning it and *what* you aim to accomplish. Are you looking to streamline multiple email accounts into one place? Do you want a tool that offers enhanced security for sensitive communication? Or maybe you need better organization for managing projects and teams. Identifying your specific goals helps shape your approach, as you'll know what features and functions to prioritize.

For example, if productivity is your main objective, focus on Thunderbird's advanced email sorting and task management features. If security is paramount, learning about encryption and privacy settings becomes essential. Having clear goals will keep you motivated and give you a sense of direction, making the learning process smoother and more rewarding.

2. Adopting a Growth Mindset

A productive learning experience is rooted in a growth mindset—the belief that skills can be developed through dedication, practice, and patience. Thunderbird, like any new tool, may have features or settings that seem complex initially, but this doesn't mean they're insurmountable. Adopting a growth mindset means welcoming challenges and viewing setbacks as learning opportunities. Every time you encounter a feature you don't understand or a task that seems complicated, remember that persistence and experimentation are part of the learning journey.

A growth mindset also encourages curiosity. Rather than focusing solely on what you need immediately, consider exploring Thunderbird's diverse features and options. This open approach can reveal functionalities that enhance your experience or inspire new ways of using the tool that you may not have considered.

3. Starting with the Basics and Building Up

One of the biggest pitfalls when learning new software is the temptation to rush into advanced features before mastering the basics. Thunderbird has a wealth of advanced settings and customization options, but building a strong foundation is essential for long-term productivity. Start with fundamental tasks like setting up email accounts, navigating the interface, and understanding the inbox organization. Familiarize yourself with core features such as sending and receiving emails, managing contacts, and setting up basic filters for sorting messages.

Once you're comfortable with these basics, gradually move on to more complex tasks like configuring message rules, creating email templates, or exploring add-ons and customization. This layered approach to learning ensures that you don't feel overwhelmed by too many features at once, making it easier to retain information and apply what you've learned effectively.

4. Embracing Customization as a Learning Tool

Thunderbird is known for its high degree of customizability, offering users control over everything from layout and themes to specific behaviors of the email client. While this can be a powerful advantage, it also requires a mindset of experimentation. Customization isn't about making Thunderbird "look cool" but rather about adapting it to work better for *you*. Take the time to explore how the customization options can enhance your productivity.

For example, if you're overwhelmed by a full inbox, consider setting up filters and folders to keep emails organized automatically. If you prefer certain colors or a layout that emphasizes particular elements, try different themes or interface adjustments. Think of customization as an active part of your learning process—experimenting with settings and layouts can often lead to a deeper understanding of Thunderbird's functionality and give you a workspace tailored to your workflow.

5. Setting Aside Dedicated Learning Time

Learning any software requires time, and Thunderbird is no different. Rather than trying to absorb everything in one sitting, set aside regular intervals dedicated solely to learning and experimenting with Thunderbird. By devoting focused, intentional time to learn, you'll absorb information better and feel less overwhelmed.

You might want to start with short daily or weekly sessions, focusing on one or two new features or tasks each time. Gradual exposure not only improves retention but also prevents burnout, allowing you to maintain a productive and motivated attitude. Remember, productivity tools like Thunderbird should ultimately save you time and enhance your workflow. Investing a little time now to learn it thoroughly can pay off significantly in the long run.

6. Emphasizing Problem-Solving and Resourcefulness

A productive mindset includes problem-solving and resourcefulness, especially when faced with features or functions that seem unclear. Thunderbird, being open-source, has an active community and extensive online resources. Embracing a resourceful mindset means utilizing these supports—consulting forums, reading documentation, or even watching tutorial videos.

For instance, Mozilla's support site offers guides and articles covering everything from basic setup to advanced troubleshooting. Third-party tutorials, video walkthroughs, and user communities like Reddit's Thunderbird forum can also be valuable resources when you encounter specific challenges. Building resourcefulness as you learn Thunderbird fosters independence, reducing frustration and enabling you to solve problems efficiently.

7. Being Patient with Your Progress

Learning any new software can feel like a slow process, especially one as feature-rich as Thunderbird. Remember that mastering the platform takes time, and it's okay if you don't immediately become an expert. Celebrate small victories, like setting up your first email filter or successfully importing contacts. Every step forward is progress.

Patience is especially important when you encounter unexpected setbacks. Perhaps an add-on didn't function as expected, or an email rule didn't apply correctly. These moments, while sometimes frustrating, are a natural part of learning. Be patient with your progress and treat each issue as an opportunity to deepen your understanding of Thunderbird.

8. Applying What You Learn to Real-World Scenarios

To solidify your learning, apply what you're learning about Thunderbird to real-world tasks. For instance, if you manage a project that requires frequent communication, set up filters and tags to categorize emails by project or client. Or, if security is a concern, explore Thunderbird's encryption features with test emails to better understand how they work.

By integrating Thunderbird into your actual workflow, you're reinforcing your knowledge and seeing firsthand how the features improve your productivity. This real-world application not only enhances your skills but also makes learning feel relevant and purposeful, boosting both motivation and satisfaction.

Final Thoughts: Cultivating a Productive Mindset

Approaching Thunderbird with the right mindset can transform your learning experience from a task into an opportunity for growth. By understanding your goals, maintaining a growth mindset, and breaking down your learning into manageable steps, you'll find Thunderbird more accessible and rewarding. Remember, Thunderbird is designed to make email management simpler, more secure, and tailored to your needs. Taking the time to approach it with patience, curiosity, and an open mind will allow you to fully unlock its potential and integrate it as a valuable tool in your productivity arsenal.

V. INTRODUCTION TO SMART DATA ANALYSIS

Leveraging Thunderbird for Effective Data Management and Analysis

While Mozilla Thunderbird is widely known as a reliable, secure, and customizable email client, it also possesses powerful features that can support smart data management and analysis. For users handling a high volume of emails or those who rely on email as a primary means of communication for business or research, Thunderbird can become a highly effective data management tool. By tapping into Thunderbird's organizational, filtering, and search capabilities, users can streamline data organization, analyze communication patterns, and enhance productivity.

In this chapter, we'll look at how Thunderbird can support smart data analysis by optimizing the way you organize, manage, and interpret email data.

1. Understanding the Role of Data Analysis in Email Management

Data analysis in email management involves organizing and examining the information contained within emails—such as message content, sender details, and communication patterns—to derive insights that can improve productivity and decision-making. Thunderbird's powerful sorting, filtering, and search tools make it possible to analyze email data in meaningful ways, helping users gain a clearer understanding of their communication trends, identify patterns, and respond to key insights.

For instance, professionals who work in customer service, sales, or project management often rely on email data to track client needs, monitor response times, and analyze common queries. Researchers may use email analysis to categorize communications from various collaborators or data sources. By taking advantage of Thunderbird's tools, users can organize this data in a structured way that supports easy analysis, helping them make more informed decisions and streamline their workflows.

2. Using Tags and Folders for Data Categorization

Thunderbird offers robust tagging and folder organization features that help users categorize and segment email data efficiently. Tags allow you to label emails based on categories such as "Urgent," "Follow-Up," "Client," "Project X," or any custom tags you create. This functionality is incredibly useful for sorting large volumes of data into manageable categories, especially if you frequently receive emails on diverse topics or from different sources.

For example, if you receive emails related to different clients or projects, you can create tags to reflect these categories. Once tagged, emails can be filtered or sorted to quickly access all messages related to a specific category. Combined with Thunderbird's folder structure, where emails can be organized into hierarchical folders and subfolders, tags enable a layered approach to email categorization. This approach supports smart data management, as you can quickly locate specific emails and analyze trends within each tag or folder.

3. Automating Data Organization with Message Filters

Thunderbird's message filters enable users to automate the organization of incoming and outgoing emails based on preset conditions. For instance, you can create filters to automatically move emails from certain senders into designated folders, apply tags to specific keywords, or archive messages after a certain period. This automation is invaluable for reducing clutter and organizing emails efficiently, allowing you to focus on the data most relevant to your work without manually sorting every message.

Filters can also help you create structured datasets for analysis. For instance, you might create filters to isolate all emails related to a specific client or project, compiling them into a dedicated folder. From there, it's easy to track conversation histories, identify frequently discussed topics, or analyze response times. Filters can be customized based on various criteria, such as sender, recipient, subject line, keywords, or even date ranges, giving you control over how data is categorized and enabling a more systematic approach to data analysis.

4. Enhanced Search Capabilities for Data Retrieval

Thunderbird's search function is a powerful tool for data analysis, as it allows users to locate specific emails or sets of emails based on a wide array of search parameters. The search bar supports advanced filters, enabling users to search by criteria such as sender, recipient, subject, attachment presence, tags, and keywords within the email body. Additionally, Thunderbird offers a search results window that displays messages in a list or threaded view, which can help you analyze the context and flow of conversations.

For users engaged in data analysis, Thunderbird's search function is especially useful for retrieving emails that match specific criteria. For example, you might search for emails sent within a particular date range to understand weekly or monthly communication trends, or search by a keyword to analyze discussions related to a particular project or issue. Thunderbird also supports saved searches, allowing users to save frequently used search parameters for easy access, which is helpful for monitoring ongoing projects or analyzing communication data over time.

5. Analyzing Communication Patterns

By combining Thunderbird's organizational tools with its search and filter functions, users can begin to analyze their email communication patterns. Analyzing factors such as response times, message frequencies, and sender distribution can offer insights into work habits and help identify areas for improvement.

For example, analyzing the frequency of emails from certain contacts can reveal which clients, team members, or projects require the most attention. Response times to specific senders can highlight how efficiently you're addressing high-priority communications. Patterns such as recurring keywords or phrases may indicate the types of inquiries or issues that arise most often, guiding improvements in documentation or communication practices.

Thunderbird's tools for sorting by date and sender can also be used to create a timeline of interactions, which is especially useful for project-based work where tracking the progression of communications is essential. These insights allow for a more data-driven approach to email management, leading to better time management and more focused attention on priority tasks.

6. Exporting and Archiving Data for Long-Term Analysis

Thunderbird offers options for exporting and archiving email data, making it easier to manage data over the long term and use it for retrospective analysis. Archiving older emails helps reduce inbox clutter while keeping historical data accessible for reference. Thunderbird allows users to set up automated archiving, which can organize emails by year, sender, or other criteria, creating a structured archive that's easy to navigate.

Exporting emails is another useful feature for users who wish to analyze data outside of Thunderbird, perhaps using external software like Excel or data analysis tools. Emails can be exported in various formats, preserving important metadata like timestamps and sender information. This data can then be transformed into structured datasets, making it possible to conduct deeper analysis and generate reports, which can be valuable for both business insights and personal productivity assessments.

7. Leveraging Add-Ons for Advanced Analysis

Thunderbird's extensibility allows users to install add-ons that enhance its capabilities for data management and analysis. There are a variety of add-ons available that can assist with everything from exporting emails to visualizing communication data. For instance, some add-ons support enhanced tagging, custom reports, and even integration with project management or CRM systems, allowing Thunderbird to function as part of a larger data management ecosystem.

For those who need more specialized analysis tools, add-ons like "ThunderStats" provide analytics within Thunderbird, showing data like average response times, daily email volume, and the most frequent contacts. Integrating Thunderbird with add-ons and other software platforms opens up even more possibilities for smart data analysis, making it a flexible solution that can be tailored to individual or business needs.

Final Thoughts: Thunderbird as a Data Analysis Tool

While many view email as just a communication tool, Thunderbird demonstrates that email can also serve as a valuable source of data and insight. Through smart data analysis, users can harness Thunderbird's powerful features to manage information, analyze communication patterns, and make more informed decisions. Whether you're a professional seeking to optimize client communications, a researcher managing large volumes of email data, or simply a user wanting to improve productivity, Thunderbird offers the tools and flexibility needed to achieve effective data management.

By approaching email management with a mindset for analysis, Thunderbird users can go beyond inbox organization, turning their email data into actionable insights. Through thoughtful use of tags, filters, search tools, and add-ons, Thunderbird can be transformed into a smart data analysis tool that supports long-term productivity and information management.

VI. USING EXCEL WITH THUNDERBIRD

Integrating Excel Skills with Thunderbird for Enhanced Productivity

Mozilla Thunderbird, a powerful and customizable email client, is often used by those who need efficient and organized communication. When combined with Microsoft Excel—a tool renowned for its data management and analysis capabilities—Thunderbird can serve as the cornerstone of a highly productive digital workflow. Integrating these two tools allows users to manage email data, perform detailed analysis, track communication patterns, and streamline reporting tasks. Whether you're a project manager, a data analyst, or a freelancer, using Excel alongside Thunderbird can unlock powerful productivity gains.

1. Why Integrate Excel with Thunderbird?

Email data often contains valuable information that, if analyzed properly, can lead to actionable insights. From tracking the frequency of client communications to analyzing response times and identifying common inquiries, email data has many hidden insights that can improve productivity and workflow. Excel is a natural partner to Thunderbird for handling this type of data, as it offers robust data manipulation, sorting, and visualization tools.

By exporting email data from Thunderbird into Excel, users can turn raw email information into structured datasets, making it easier to analyze, visualize, and act on trends. Excel can help summarize complex data and create visual reports, making it an essential tool for users who need to manage large volumes of communication or track various metrics related to their email correspondence.

2. Exporting Thunderbird Data for Excel Analysis

To begin using Excel with Thunderbird, you first need to export the data you want to analyze. Thunderbird allows emails to be exported into formats like CSV or EML, which can then be imported into Excel. While there are different methods for exporting emails, some users find it helpful to use Thunderbird add-ons designed specifically for data export, such as "ImportExportTools NG." This add-on streamlines the process, allowing users to select entire folders or specific date ranges for export and choose CSV format, which is ideal for Excel analysis.

Once the email data is in CSV format, it can be easily opened in Excel. Here, the data appears as rows and columns, with fields like "Date," "Sender," "Subject," "Body Text," and "Recipient" represented in separate columns. By structuring your email data this way, you gain control over sorting, filtering, and analyzing it based on any criteria important to you.

3. Organizing Email Data in Excel for Better Insights

Once your email data is in Excel, the next step is to organize it for meaningful analysis. Excel's data organization tools—such as sorting, filtering, and conditional formatting—make it easy to clean up and categorize data, enhancing your ability to interpret it effectively.

Sorting and Filtering: Start by sorting your email data by columns like "Sender" or "Date" to identify specific patterns, such as which clients email you most frequently or during what times communication peaks. Filtering allows you to view only specific segments of data, such as emails from a particular project or time period, making it easier to focus on specific inquiries or communication history.

Conditional Formatting: Conditional formatting is a powerful feature for highlighting important information. For instance, you could use it to color-code emails from high-priority clients, mark overdue responses in red, or highlight emails with specific keywords. Conditional formatting makes it easy to identify key trends or anomalies at a glance, which is invaluable for prioritizing tasks and improving response times.

Pivot Tables: For more advanced users, pivot tables are an excellent way to summarize and analyze large volumes of email data. Pivot tables allow you to quickly group data by categories, such as monthly email counts, most common senders, or topics frequently discussed. This level of analysis can provide insights into how you're spending your time, which projects are most communication-heavy, and where your workflow could be optimized.

4. Analyzing Communication Patterns with Excel's Data Tools

Excel's data analysis tools allow you to extract patterns from your email data that can be used to optimize workflows. For instance, if you find that a particular client tends to email during specific times or needs frequent follow-ups, you can adjust your scheduling to improve responsiveness.

Frequency Analysis: By grouping emails by date and time, you can analyze daily, weekly, or monthly email volumes. This analysis can help you identify peak times when you receive the most emails, allowing you to allocate time for focused email management during those periods.

Response Time Tracking: If response times are important in your role, Excel can help you calculate average response times by subtracting the timestamp of the received email from the timestamp of your reply. By analyzing response times across clients or projects, you can identify areas for improvement and set benchmarks to increase efficiency.

Keyword Analysis: Excel's "Text to Columns" feature and filters can be used to isolate keywords or specific phrases from your emails. This can be useful for identifying common questions, tracking project-specific language, or flagging customer service issues. By tagging and tracking keywords, you can gain insights into what topics are most frequently discussed or identify recurring issues that need attention.

5. Creating Visual Reports for Communication Analysis

Excel's charting and visualization capabilities make it a powerful tool for presenting insights derived from email data. Creating visual reports can help communicate findings to stakeholders or provide a snapshot of your communication patterns at a glance.

Charts and Graphs: Bar charts, line graphs, and pie charts are effective for visualizing email trends over time. For example, a bar chart could show the number of emails sent per client each month, while a line graph might depict response times across different projects. Visual reports make it easier to digest complex data, helping you quickly spot trends or areas where improvements are needed.

Dashboards: For those looking to regularly track and analyze communication data, creating an Excel dashboard can be a time-saving solution. A dashboard consolidates key metrics, such as email frequency, response times, and contact volume, into a single view. By using Excel's chart and pivot table features, you can design a customized dashboard that updates as new data is added, making it easy to monitor trends in real-time.

6. Automating Data Updates with Excel and Thunderbird

One of the biggest advantages of combining Excel with Thunderbird is the potential for automation. With tools like macros in Excel or automated exports in

Thunderbird, users can streamline data transfer and update their analysis with minimal manual effort.

For example, you could set up a recurring data export from Thunderbird that captures weekly or monthly email data. Then, by linking your exported data to Excel's data sources, you can refresh your analysis without re-importing data manually each time. This setup allows you to keep your insights up-to-date effortlessly, providing you with real-time data for decision-making and planning.

7. Integrating Thunderbird Data with Broader Business Analysis

In addition to personal productivity, Thunderbird's data can be incorporated into broader business analyses when combined with Excel. For project managers, Thunderbird's data—once organized in Excel—can be integrated into reports tracking project progress, client interactions, or resource allocation. Sales teams might use this data to monitor customer interactions, measure response rates, or identify high-value contacts based on communication frequency.

Since Excel is compatible with a wide range of business tools and reporting software, Thunderbird's email data can be integrated with CRM systems, financial analysis platforms, or task management tools. This integration allows you to enrich your overall business data with communication insights, providing a more comprehensive view of project health, client relationships, and team productivity.

Final Thoughts: Leveraging Excel with Thunderbird for Enhanced Productivity

Integrating Excel with Thunderbird transforms email management into a powerful data analysis activity. Excel's data manipulation and visualization capabilities complement Thunderbird's robust email management tools, allowing users to turn raw communication data into actionable insights. By effectively exporting, organizing, analyzing, and visualizing email data, you can not only manage communication more efficiently but also uncover trends and optimize your workflow.

Whether you're tracking response times, analyzing customer interactions, or presenting communication metrics, the Thunderbird-Excel integration can help you take email management to the next level. By establishing a streamlined workflow between the two tools, you can improve productivity, maintain better control over email data, and make more informed decisions—all while saving time and enhancing organization.

VII. LOOKING AHEAD: THE FUTURE OF THUNDERBIRD

Potential Developments and What's Next for Thunderbird Users

Mozilla Thunderbird has been a mainstay in the email client world for almost two decades, evolving to meet the needs of users and keeping pace with advancements in digital communication. As a free, open-source software, Thunderbird is shaped not only by its core team but also by a vibrant community of contributors. This collaborative spirit, combined with a focus on privacy, customization, and user empowerment, positions Thunderbird to continue as a key player in email management. As technology advances and user needs grow, Thunderbird is poised to embrace several new trends and developments that will enhance its functionality and relevance.

1. Modernization of the User Interface

One of the most anticipated developments for Thunderbird is a comprehensive modernization of its user interface (UI). The current design, while functional and familiar to long-term users, can appear dated compared to contemporary email clients. An updated UI with a cleaner, more intuitive layout will improve accessibility and appeal to new users.

Future UI enhancements may include:

- **Responsive Design:** A dynamic layout that adapts seamlessly to various screen sizes, making Thunderbird more user-friendly on laptops, tablets, and mobile devices.

- **Dark Mode and Theme Customization:** While Thunderbird already has a Dark Mode, more refined customization options will allow users to tailor the appearance further, adding comfort for those who work in low-light conditions.

- **Streamlined Navigation:** Expect more fluid navigation, with essential tools placed at the user's fingertips. Reducing clutter and consolidating frequently used features into a single interface could enhance user experience and reduce the learning curve for beginners.

2. Integration with Cloud Services

In today's interconnected digital landscape, integration with cloud services has become a priority for users who rely on cloud storage and collaboration tools. The future of Thunderbird likely involves more seamless connectivity with popular cloud platforms, such as Google Drive, Dropbox, OneDrive, and other file-sharing services. This integration would make it easier for users to attach, share, and access documents directly from the cloud without needing to download and re-upload files manually.

Cloud integration could also improve collaboration for users working in teams by allowing them to save, organize, and share emails and attachments directly through Thunderbird. Additionally, integration with popular productivity suites (such as Microsoft 365 or Google Workspace) would enhance Thunderbird's appeal as a comprehensive communication and productivity tool for businesses and teams.

3. Enhanced Mobile and Cross-Device Compatibility

As mobile and cross-device functionality becomes increasingly important, Thunderbird's development team is likely to focus on extending Thunderbird's compatibility with mobile devices. Although Thunderbird is currently limited to desktop environments, users frequently request a mobile version for Android and iOS. A Thunderbird mobile app would allow users to synchronize email accounts across devices, providing a unified inbox and seamless email management on the go.

Thunderbird could also benefit from improvements in synchronization between desktop and mobile versions, similar to how Firefox syncs bookmarks, history, and preferences across devices. Cross-device compatibility would make it easier for users to transition between devices without losing context, ensuring a consistent and uninterrupted workflow.

4. Expansion of Advanced Security Features

Thunderbird has built a reputation for its strong focus on privacy and security, a commitment that will likely expand in the coming years. As cybersecurity threats continue to evolve, Thunderbird's development team is expected to enhance the software's security features to keep user data safe.

Potential security advancements include:

- **Enhanced End-to-End Encryption:** Thunderbird already supports OpenPGP encryption, but future updates may streamline the encryption process to make it more accessible to less tech-savvy users. Simplified encryption processes, along with user-friendly guides, could help more users protect their communications.

- **Improved Spam and Phishing Filters:** With AI-driven spam filters becoming more common, Thunderbird may incorporate machine learning algorithms to detect spam, phishing, and malware more effectively, adapting to emerging threats in real-time.

- **Two-Factor Authentication (2FA) Integration:** While Thunderbird already supports 2FA for some email providers, expanding built-in support for additional 2FA methods (like app-based authentication or hardware tokens) would enhance overall account security.

5. More Powerful Data Analysis and Reporting Tools

Thunderbird's role as an email client can be expanded by incorporating data analysis tools, making it valuable for users interested in tracking and analyzing communication patterns. For example, business users might benefit from tools that analyze email frequency, response times, or categorize emails by priority. Adding data analysis features directly within Thunderbird could turn it into an all-in-one tool for communication tracking and management.

Possible data analysis developments include:

- **Analytics Dashboard:** A built-in dashboard displaying metrics like response rates, email volumes, most active contacts, and average response times.

- **Customizable Reporting:** Tools that allow users to generate reports based on communication data, which could be helpful for businesses to analyze team productivity and customer interaction trends.

- **Integration with Other Data Tools:** For advanced users, Thunderbird could offer integration with tools like Microsoft Power BI or Google Data Studio, allowing email data to be exported and analyzed alongside other business metrics.

6. Improved Calendar and Task Management Features

Thunderbird's calendar functionality, known as the Lightning add-on, is already popular among users for task and schedule management. However, as productivity tools evolve, Thunderbird has the opportunity to enhance its calendar and task features, transforming itself into a more comprehensive productivity suite.

Some anticipated improvements could include:

- **Task Assignment and Collaboration:** Tools for assigning and sharing tasks with team members, including task updates and status notifications.

- **Enhanced Calendar Syncing:** More seamless synchronization with other popular calendar services, such as Google Calendar, Outlook Calendar, and Apple iCal, making it easier for users to manage appointments across platforms.

- **Customizable Reminders and Notifications:** Flexible notification options that allow users to set multiple reminders or receive alerts on different devices, enhancing their ability to stay organized.

7. Artificial Intelligence and Machine Learning Capabilities

AI and machine learning are rapidly transforming email clients, helping to automate repetitive tasks and personalize the user experience. Thunderbird could integrate machine learning to streamline common tasks like email sorting, filtering, and even composing.

Some AI-driven features that could be introduced include:

- **Smart Sorting and Filtering:** Machine learning algorithms that adapt to user behavior, automatically categorizing or tagging emails based on patterns detected in user interactions.

- **Predictive Text and Response Suggestions:** AI-powered response suggestions or predictive text to speed up email composition, similar to features seen in Gmail's Smart Compose.

- **Personalized Email Prioritization:** By analyzing patterns in email interactions, Thunderbird could prioritize certain emails, making sure the most relevant messages are seen first.

8. Increasing Integration with Third-Party Tools and APIs

As businesses and individuals continue to use an array of productivity tools, future versions of Thunderbird will likely focus on integration with third-party applications through APIs. This integration could include compatibility with CRM systems, project management platforms like Asana or Trello, and file storage solutions.

Such integrations could streamline workflows, enabling users to access data from various systems directly within Thunderbird, making it a versatile hub for productivity and communication. By integrating with other business tools, Thunderbird can broaden its utility beyond email, potentially becoming an essential tool in users' daily workflows.

Final Thoughts: The Future of Thunderbird

Looking ahead, Thunderbird's development roadmap reflects its commitment to providing a secure, flexible, and modern email experience. By focusing on UI updates, cloud and mobile integration, enhanced security, data analysis tools, and AI capabilities, Thunderbird aims to remain relevant and useful for a wide range of users—from individual email users to business teams with complex communication needs.

As these potential developments unfold, Thunderbird is likely to continue thriving as a trusted, open-source alternative in the email client market, consistently adapting to the evolving needs of its user base. With its commitment to privacy, customization, and community-driven development, Thunderbird is well-positioned to stay at the forefront of email and productivity solutions for years to come.

CHAPTER 2: INSTALLATION AND INITIAL SETUP

This chapter will guide you through the installation and configuration of Thunderbird Mail on your computer. Prior to installation, it is important to ensure that your computer meets the system requirements.

2.1 SYSTEM REQUIREMENTS

Before you start in stalling Thunderbird Mail, you should make sure that your computer meets the necessary system requirements. The requirements vary depending on the operating system, but in general the minimum requirements are as follows:

- **Operating system:** Windows 10 or later, macOS X 10.15 or later, or Linux (distributions such as Ubuntu, Fedora, Debian, openSUSE etc.)
- **Processor**: 1 GHz or faster
- **Memory** (RAM): 51 2 MB (recommended: 2 GB or more)
- **Free hard disk space:** At least 200 MB for the installation, additional storage space for your e-mails and files
- **Screen resolution:** at least 1024 x 768 pixels
- **Internet connection:** Required for downloading, updating, and sending/receiving e-mails.

Please be advised that the performance of Thunderbird Mail can be enhanced by ensuring that the system meets the necessary requirements. For instance, if you manage a substantial volume of emails or have installed numerous add-ons and extensions, additional RAM and a faster processor may be beneficial.

Please ensure that your computer meets the system requirements before continuing. The following sections will guide you through the process of downloading, installing, and configuring Thunderbird Mail.

2.2 DOWNLOAD AND INSTALLATION

Once you have verified that your computer meets the system requirements, you may proceed with the download and installation of Thunderbird Mail. Please refer to the instructions below for your particular operating system.

2.2.3 WINDOWS AND MACOS:

[Screenshot of Mozilla Thunderbird Setup Wizard welcome screen]

1. Please visit the official Thunderbird website at https://www.thunderbird.net.

The website is designed to automatically recognize your operating system and provide you with the corresponding download link.

2. click on the "***Download***" button to start the download. The downloaded file will be provided in the installation format for your operating system (e.g.,.exe for Windows or .dmg for macOS).
3. navigate to the location of the downloaded file and double-click on it to start the installation process.
4. follow the instructions of the installation wizard to install Thunderbird Mail. As a rule, you must select the installation path and a few options before you complete the installation.

2.2.4 LINUX

1. The installation of Thunderbird under Linux varies depending on the distribution used. For most distributions, including Ubuntu, Debian, and Fedora, you can install Thunderbird via the terminal or the Software Manager.
2. To install Thunderbird via the terminal, open a terminal window and enter the appropriate command for your distribution:
- Ubuntu/Debian: / Debian: "***sudo apt-get install thunderbird***"
- Fedora: "***sudo dnf install thunderbird***"

- openSUSE: "*sudo zypper install thunderbird*"
3. The package manager will download the required packages and install Thunderbird Mail on your system.

After the successful installation of Thunderbird Mail, you can now continue with the setup of your e-mail account.

2.3 USING THUNDERBIRD ON A USB STICK

If you frequently switch between different computers and want to have your emails and settings with you at all times, using Thunderbird on a USB stick can be particularly useful. Here are the steps to set up Thunderbird on a USB stick:

1. Please download the Thunderbird Portable application. Please visit the PortableApps.com website and search for **"Thunderbird Portable."** Please download the installation package and save it on your computer.
2. Please refer to the instructions provided with the USB stick for details on how to install the software. Connect your USB stick to your computer. Please execute the downloaded installation file and select the USB stick as the installation location.
3. **Installation of Thunderbird:** Start Thunderbird Portable from the USB stick when the installation is complete. Now you can set up your e-mail account, just like in the normal version of Thunderbird.
4. **Use Thunderbird on other computers:** Use Thunderbird on another computer. Simply insert the USB stick into the computer and start Thunderbird Portable. All your emails and settings will be exactly as you left them.

Please be aware that using Thunderbird on a USB stick has certain limitations. Please be aware that due to the limited speed of the USB stick, access to emails and general performance may be slower. Furthermore, the data stored on the USB stick may not be as secure as on your computer unless you encrypt or employ other security measures.

2.4 ACCOUNT SETUP

Once you have successfully installed Thunderbird Mail, the next step is to set up your email account. Follow the steps below to add and configure your account in Thunderbird Mail.

1. To begin, launch Thunderbird Mail. The "***Account Setup***" will automatically open the first time you start it. If the wizard does not start automatically, you can open it manually by clicking on the hamburger menu in the top right corner > **"New Account" > "Existing Email."**

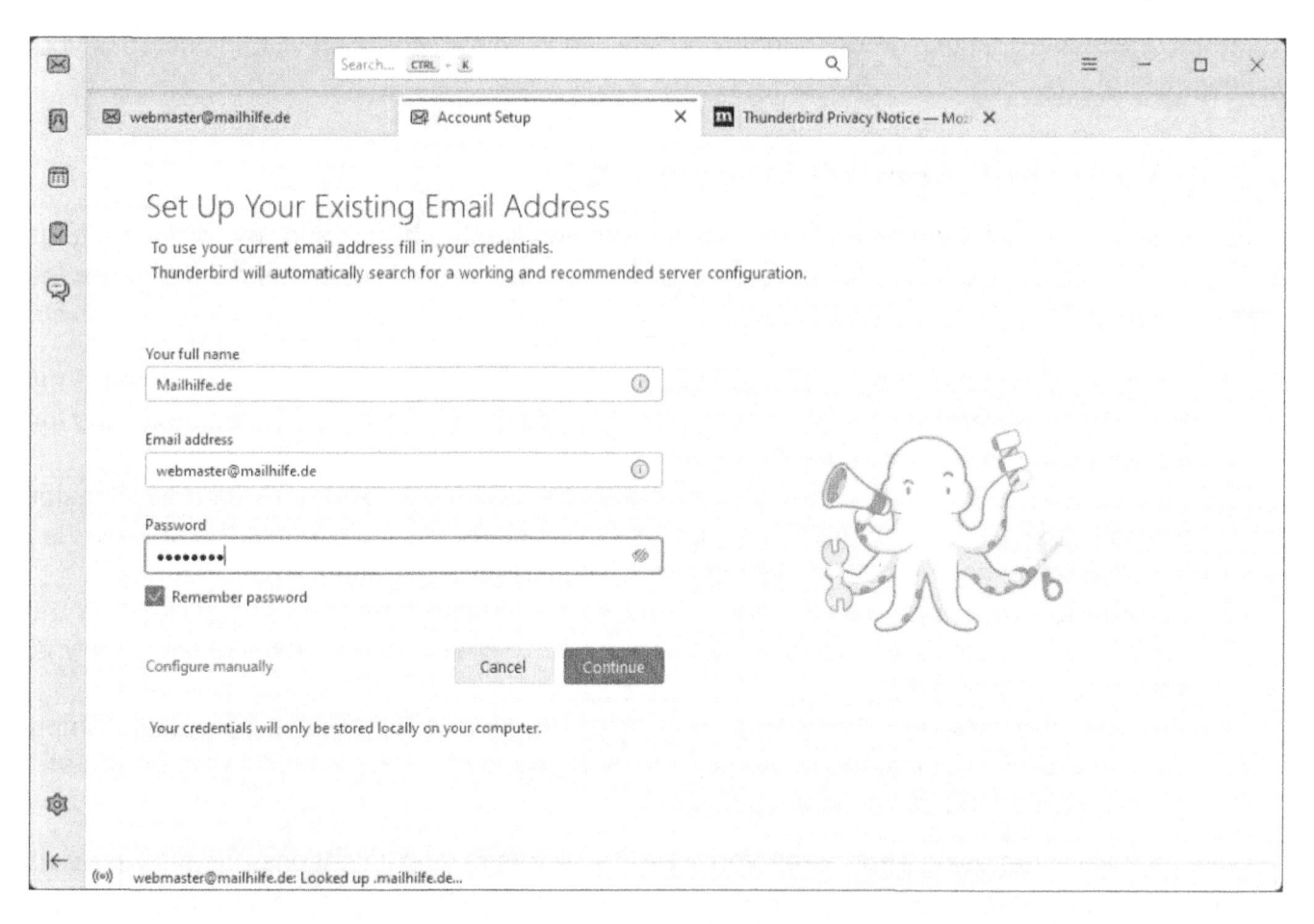

2. Please enter your email address, your name, and your password in the account wizard. The name is the display name that will appear in emails sent from this account.
3. Please click on "**Continue**." Thunderbird Mail will attempt to automatically recognize and configure the settings of your email account. In the majority of cases, this process should be successful. If Thunderbird is unable to recognize the settings automatically, you may need to select manual configuration and manually change the settings for the incoming mail server (IMAP or POP3) and the outgoing mail server (SMTP). Please contact your email provider for further assistance.

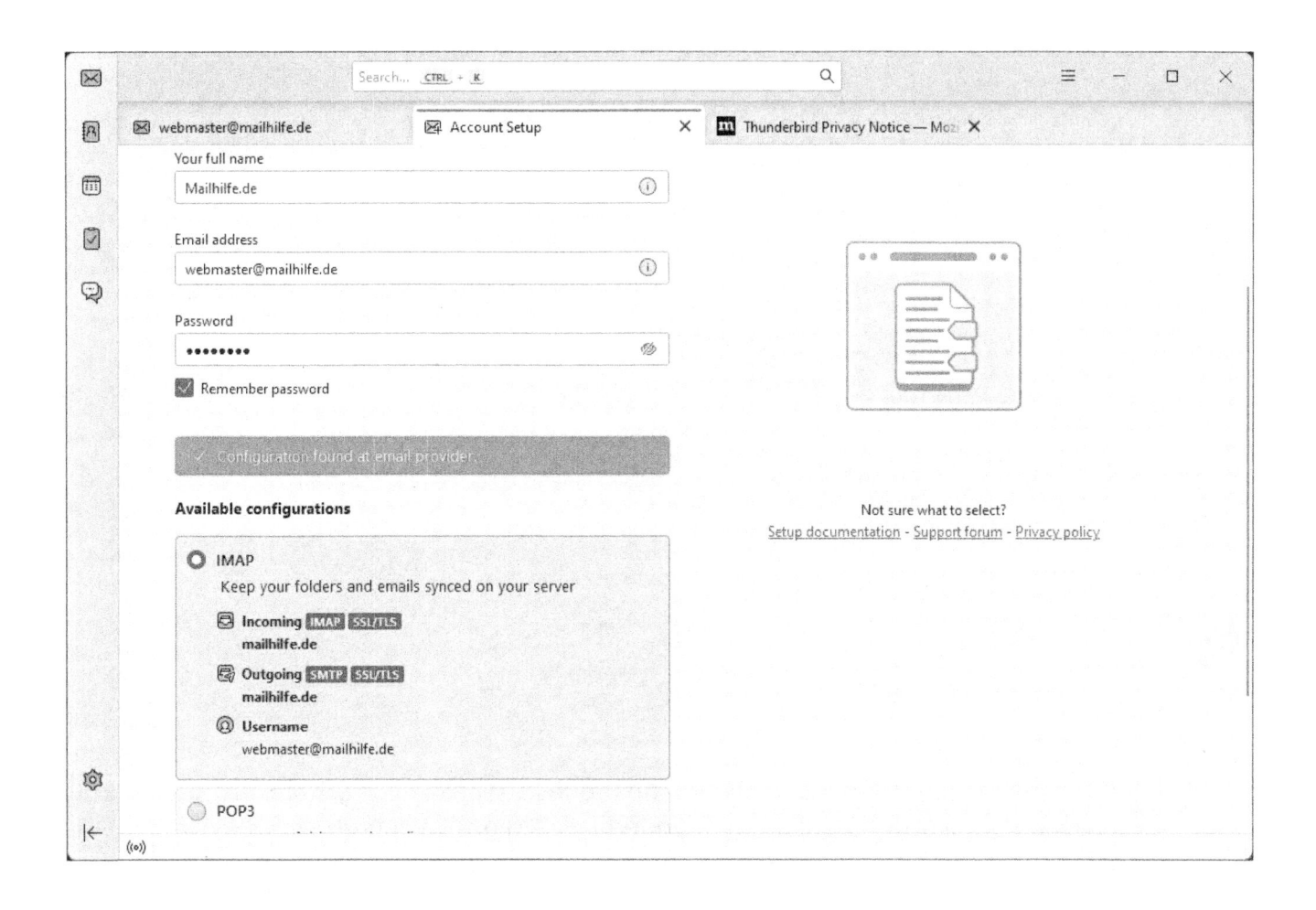

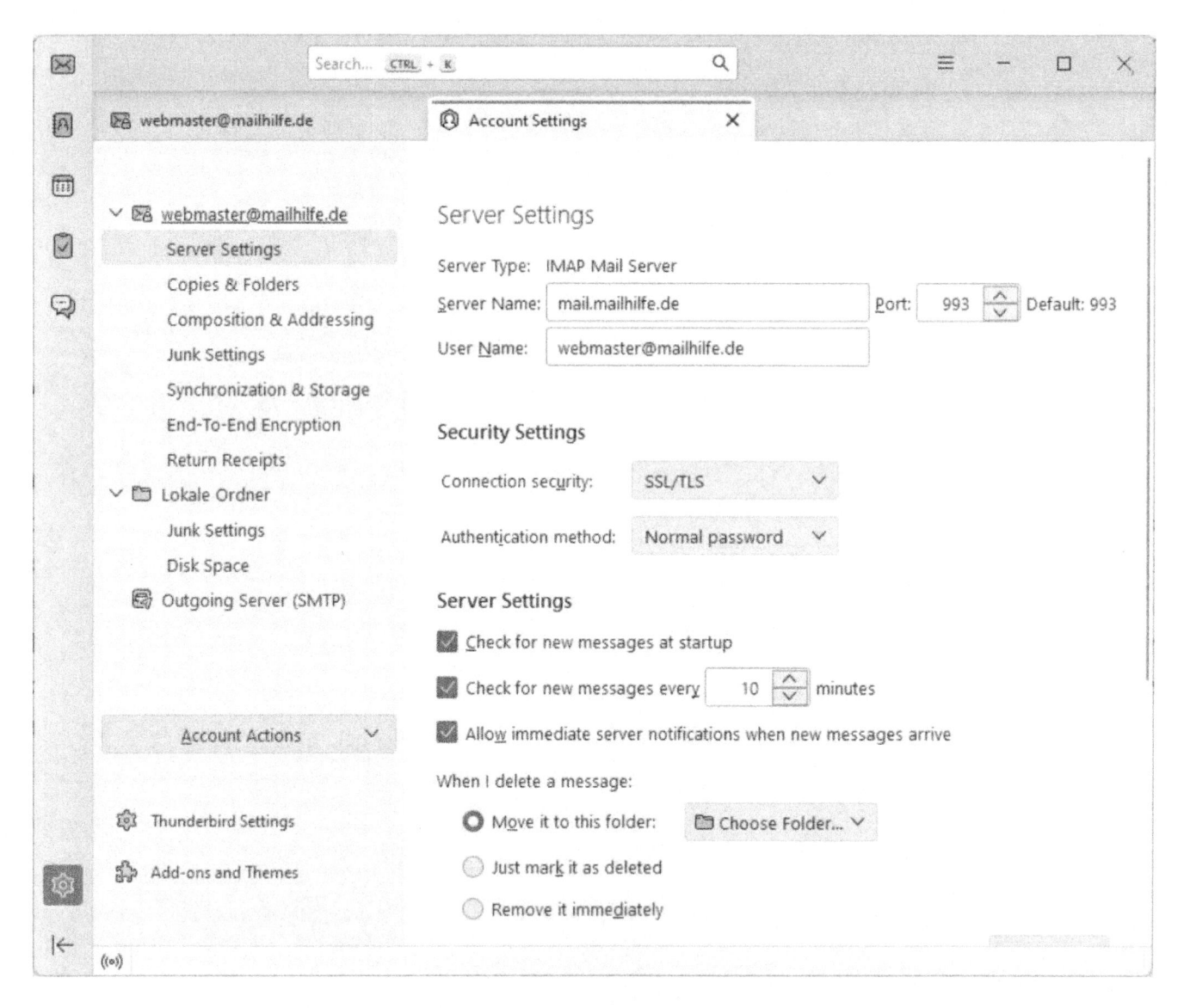

4. Once you have completed the configuration process, please click the "**Done**" button. Your email account will now be added to Thunderbird Mail and synchronized.
5. Please be advised that your emails have now been successfully imported into the Thunderbird Mail inbox. You will see the folder structure of your account on the left-hand side. You are now able to send and receive emails and utilize all the functions of Thunderbird Mail.

Should you wish to add further email accounts, please simply repeat the aforementioned steps. Thunderbird Mail offers users the ability to manage multiple email accounts simultaneously, eliminating the need to log in and out of each account individually.

CHAPTER 3: PERSONALIZATION AND CUSTOMIZATION OPTIONS

Thunderbird Mail provides numerous options for tailoring the appearance and functionality of the email client to suit your specific requirements and preferences. This chapter will teach you how to personalize and customize Thunderbird Mail to optimize your email experience.

3.1 INTERFACE DESIGN AND THEMES

Thunderbird Mail offers users the ability to customize the appearance of the client through the use of themes. Themes are visual designs that alter the colors, icons, and general style of the application. To install and use a theme, please follow these steps:

1. Open Thunderbird Mail and click on the menu icon (three horizontal bars) in the top right corner of the window.
2. Select "**Add-ons and Themes**" to display the available themes. Thunderbird offers several pre-installed themes, including "**Syste, theme", "Light,"** and "**Dark**".

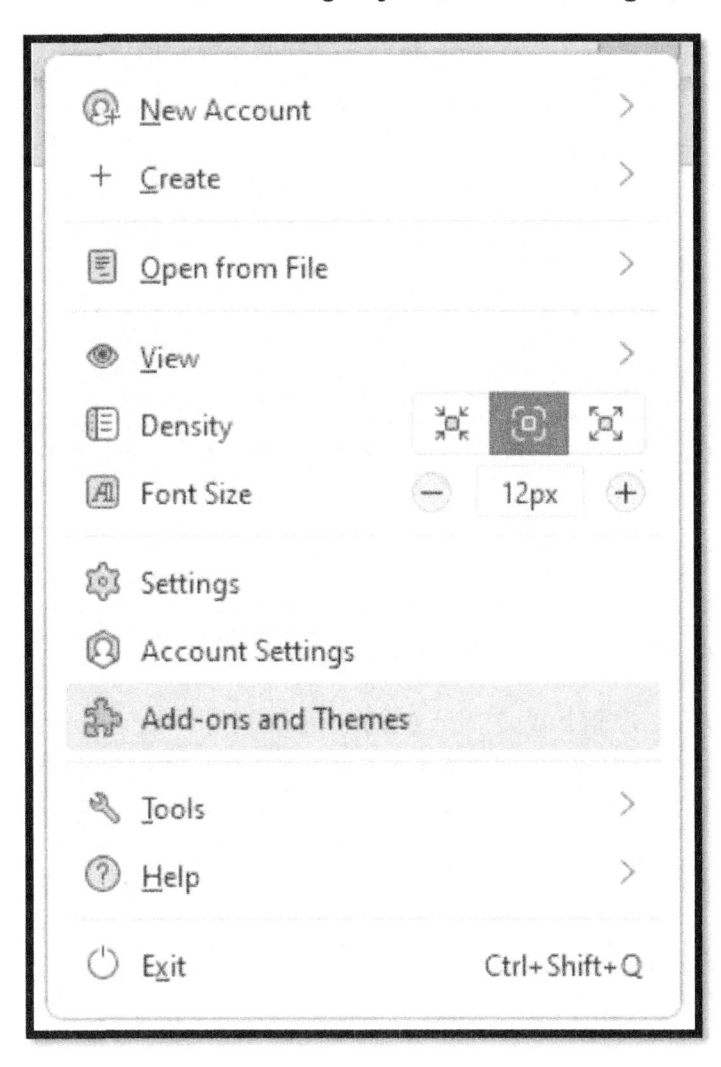

3. to browse and download more themes, click on "**Themes**" on the left-hand side. This opens the Thunderbird Add-ons Manager in the "Themes" tab.

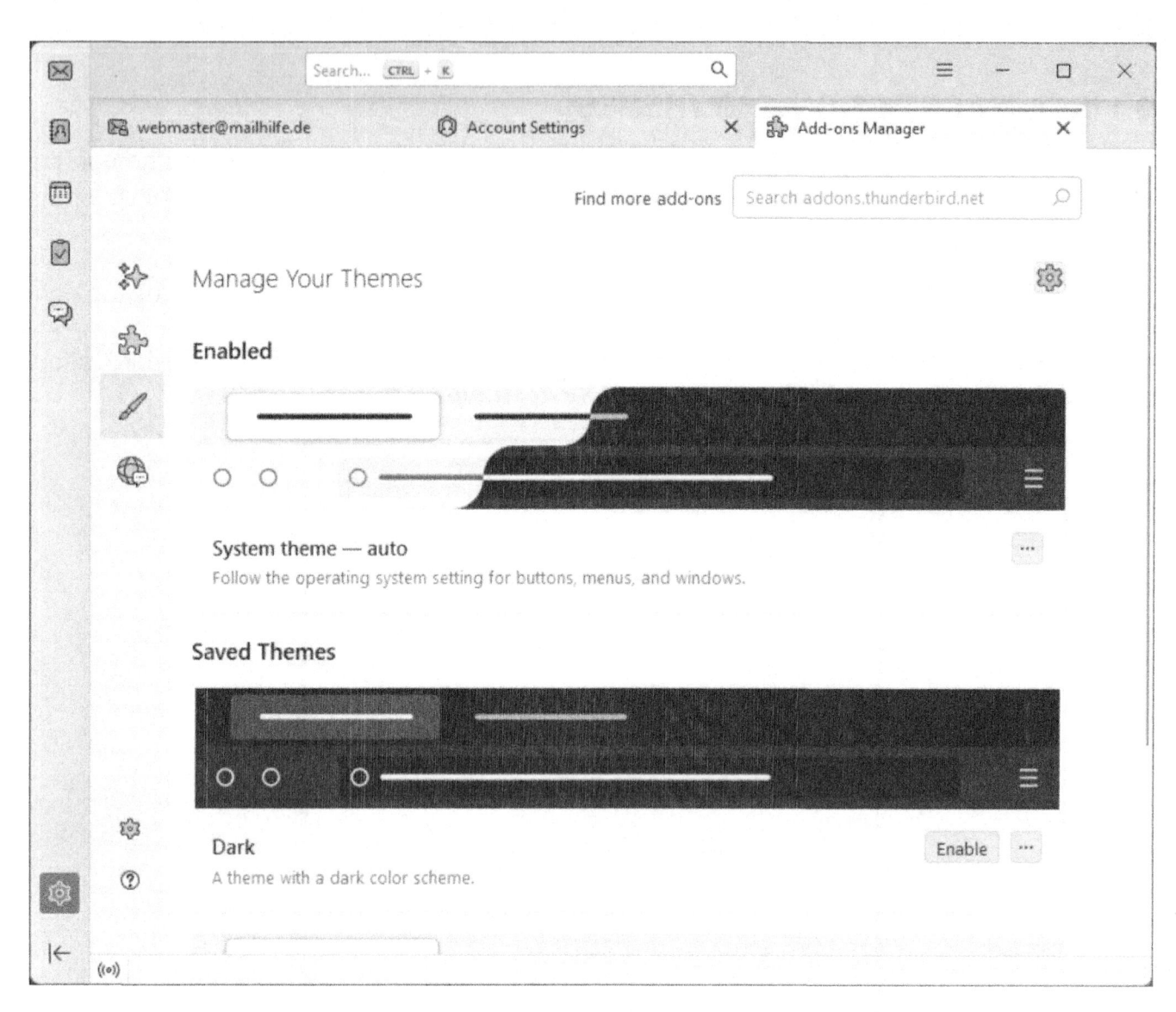

4. Enter, e.g., "**Dark Fox**" in the search bar at the top." in the search bar. All themes with the name "Dark **Fox**" will now be displayed. Click on "**Add to Thunderbird**" to download and install the desired theme. After installation, the theme will appear in the list of available themes.

Sort by:

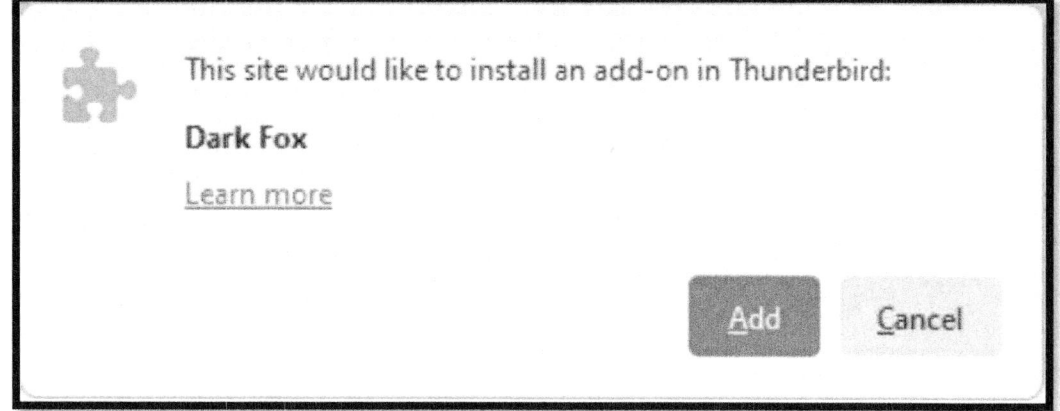

Dark Fox [FEATURED]
My dark version of the Firefox logo.
★★★★★ (608) · 17,933 users

+ Add to Thunderbird

Dark Fox 2.1
creating this persona I'd looked up to default dark fox but I've enhanced it a little
★★★★☆ (9) · 19 users

+ Add to Thunderbird

Dark Fox 7 lite
This persona adapted from Dark Fox 7, by fronzy75.
★★★★★ (11) · 12 users

+ Add to Thunderbird

Dark Fox No Logo
Edit of randomaster Dark Fox theme to remove logo.
★★★★☆ (1) · 0 users

+ Add to Thunderbird

Face Fox Dark
My simple, yet cute, rendition of the Firefox logo. On a subtly textured matte black background.
★★★★★ (17) · 15 users

+ Add to Thunderbird

This site would like to install an add-on in Thunderbird:

Dark Fox

Learn more

[Add] [Cancel]

5. To apply a theme, click on the "**Enable**" button next to the desired theme and restart Thunderbird Mail. The selected theme is now applied and changes the appearance of Thunderbird accordingly.

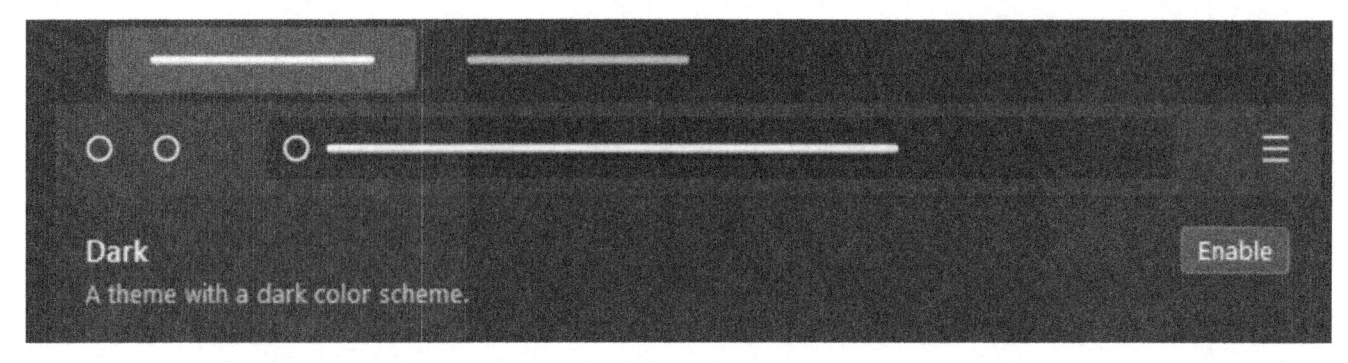

You can switch to a different theme at any time by repeating the steps above and selecting a different theme from the list. To return to the default theme, click on "**Disable**" next to the currently active theme and restart Thunderbird Mail.

3.2 CUSTOMIZING TOOLBARS AND MENUS

Thunderbird Mail offers users the flexibility to customize the toolbars and menus to align with their personal preferences and workflows. You have the option of adding, removing, or rearranging buttons to optimize access to frequently used functions. Please follow the steps below to customize the toolbars and menus in Thunderbird Mail.

1. Open Thunderbird Mail and click on the menu icon (three horizontal bars) in the top right corner of the window.
2. Select "***View -> Toolbars -> Toolbar Layout***" from the menu. This opens the customization mode in which you can edit the toolbars and menus.

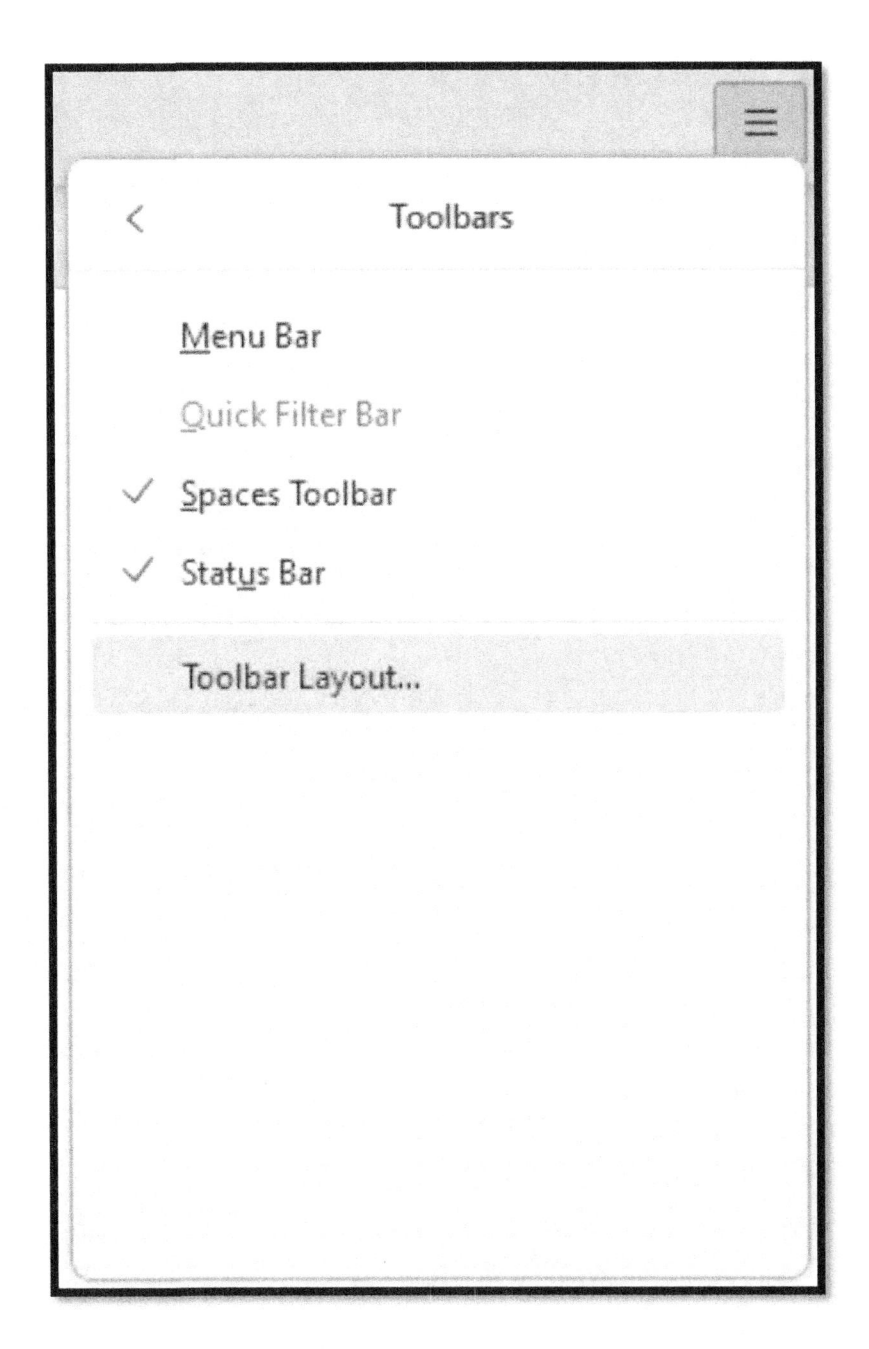

3. In customization mode, you will see all available buttons and elements that can be added to the toolbar or menu. To add a button, simply click on the desired element and drag it to the desired position in the toolbar or menu.

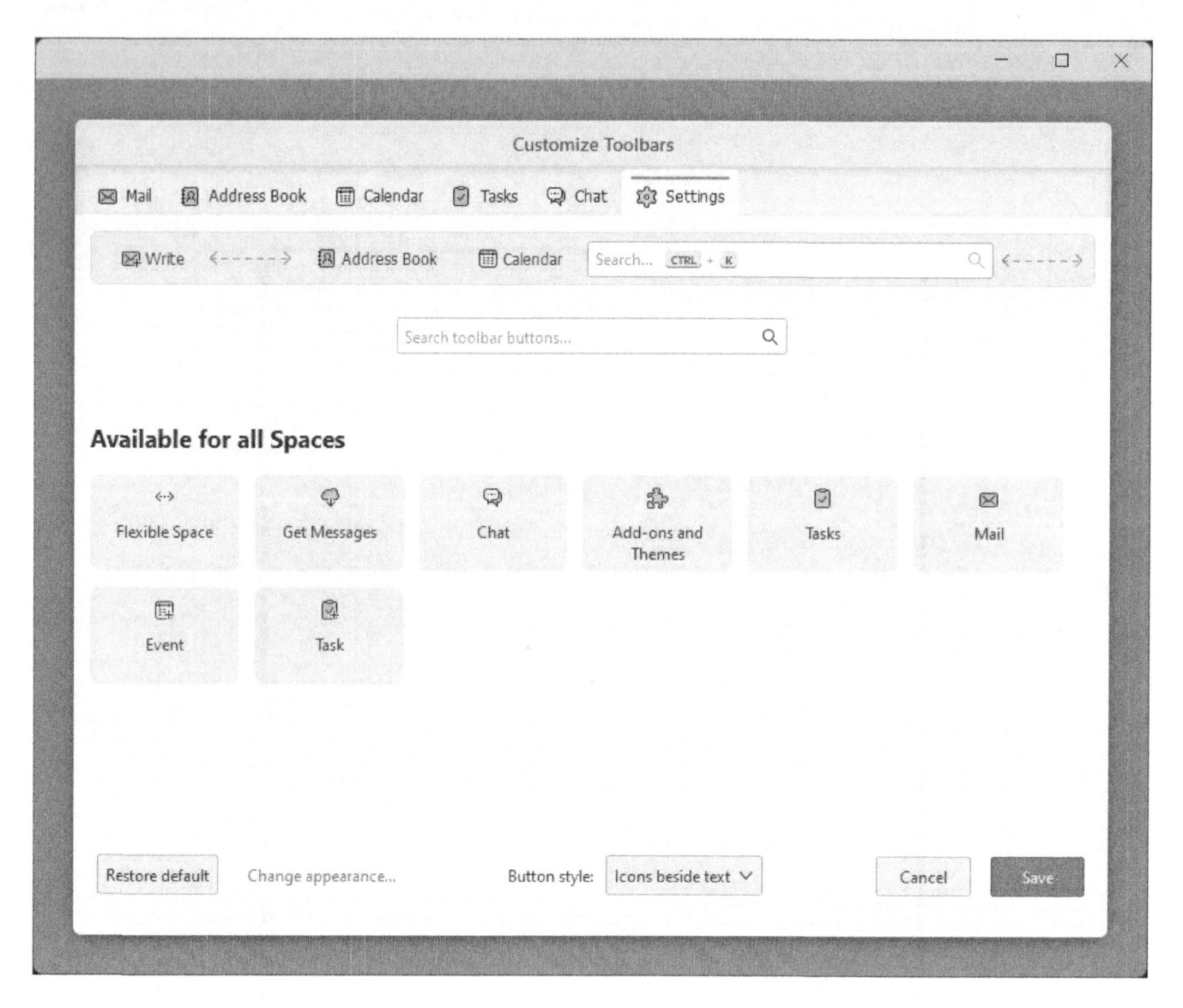

4. To remove a button from the toolbar or menu, click on the element and drag it from the toolbar or menu to the customization area.
5. You can change the order of the buttons and elements by dragging them to the desired position in the toolbar menu.
6. When you are finished, click "**Save**" in the bottom right corner of the customization window to save your changes and exit the customization mode.

By customizing your toolbars and menus to your specific needs, you can increase the efficiency of your work with Thunderbird Mail and simplify your daily email management.

3.3 KEYBOARD SHORTCUTS

Keyboard shortcuts are an efficient way to access Thunderbird Mail features and perform various actions without using the mouse. Using keyboard shortcuts can significantly increase your productivity and help you save time. Below you will find a list of the most common and useful keyboard shortcuts in Thunderbird Mail:

- **Create a new e-mail:** Ctrl + N (Windows/Linux) or Cmd + N (macOS)
- **Reply to an e-mail:** Ctrl + R (Windows/Linux) or Cmd + R (macOS)
- **Reply to all:** Ctrl + Shift + R (Windows/Linux) or Cmd + Shift + R (macOS)

- **Forward e-mail:** Ctrl + L (Windows/Linux) or Cmd + L (macOS)
- **Delete e-mail:** Del (Windows/Linux) or Cmd + Del (macOS).
- **Mark e-mail as junk:** Ctrl + Shift + J (Windows/ Linux) or Cmd + Shift + J (macOS).
- **Search e-mail:** Ctrl + F (Windows/Linux) or Cmd + F (macOS)
- **Select next e-mail:** Ctrl +. (Windows/Linux) or Cmd +. (macOS)
- **Select previous email:** Ctrl +, (Windows/Linux) or Cmd +, (macOS)
- **Save e-mail address in the address book:** Ctrl + Shift + C (Windows/Linux) or Cmd + Shift + C (macOS)
- **Open address book:** Ctrl + Shift + B (Windows/Linux) or Cmd + Shift + B (macOS).
- **Change e-mail folder:** Ctrl + Y (Windows/Linux) or Cmd + Y (MacOS).
- **Retrieve emails:** Ctrl + T (Windows/Linux) or Cmd + T (MacOS).

You can also create your own custom keyboard shortcuts by using an add-on.

"TBKeys Lite" is an extension for Thunderbird that provides a user-friendly way to customize keyboard shortcuts in the email client. With this extension, you can change, add, or remove keyboard shortcuts to increase your productivity and customize the use of Thunderbird to your personal preferences.

To use "TBKeys Lite," follow these steps:

1. Install the "TBKeys Lite" extension from the official Thunderbird Add-ons website or from a trusted provider.
2. Restart Thunderbird after the installation.
3. Open Thunderbird Mail and click on the menu icon (three horizontal bars) in the top right corner of the window. Select "***Add-ons and Themes", - > "Extensions***."
4. Go to the "***TBKeys Lite settings***" to open the extension settings.
5. In the settings of "TBKeys Lite," you can change existing keyboard shortcuts, add new keyboard shortcuts, or remove unwanted keyboard shortcuts.

![Screenshot of tbkeys-lite add-on settings in Thunderbird showing JSON configuration for key bindings]

```
{
    "j": "cmd:cmd_nextMsg",
    "k": "cmd:cmd_previousMsg",
    "o": "cmd:cmd_openMessage",
    "f": "cmd:cmd_forward",
    "#": "cmd:cmd_delete",
    "r": "cmd:cmd_reply",
    "a": "cmd:cmd_replyall",
    "x": "cmd:cmd_archive",
    "c": "func:MsgNewMessage",
    "u": "tbkeys:closeMessageAndRefresh"
}
```

6. Save your changes, and the customized shortcuts will be activated in Thunderbird.

With "TBKeys Lite," you can quickly and easily customize the keyboard shortcuts in Thunderbird to your needs to increase the efficiency of your work and improve the user experience.

By using keyboard shortcuts in Thunderbird Mail and customizing them to your needs, you can increase your work efficiency and save time by quickly accessing functions and actions.

CHAPTER 4: MANAGING YOUR EMAILS EFFECTIVELY

Efficient email management is crucial for keeping track of your communications and staying productive. Thunderbird offers a variety of features and tools to help you manage your emails. This chapter covers the various aspects of email management in Thunderbird Mail.

4.1 INBOX ORGANIZE

An effective organization of your inbox in Thunderbird Mail is essential for maintaining control of your emails and enhancing your productivity. This chapter will provide guidance on how to organize and manage your inbox in Thunderbird Mail.

4.2 FOLDER STRUCTURE

Use folders and subfolders to sort your emails by topic or project. To create a new folder, right-click on an existing folder (e.g., Inbox) and select "***New Subfolder***...". Enter a name for the folder and confirm.

4.3 FILTERS AND RULES

Filters and rules are features built into Thunderbird Mail that help users organize their emails automatically by performing certain actions based on predefined criteria. Filters and rules enable users to automate the movement of emails to folders, mark them as read or unread, delete or forward them, in accordance with their personal preferences and organizational requirements.

4.3.1 CREATING FILTERS

To create a new filter in Thunderbird Mail, proceed as follows:

1. Open Thunderbird Mail and click on the menu icon (three horizontal bars) in the top right corner of the window.
2. Select "***Tools***" and then "***Message Filters***" from the menu.

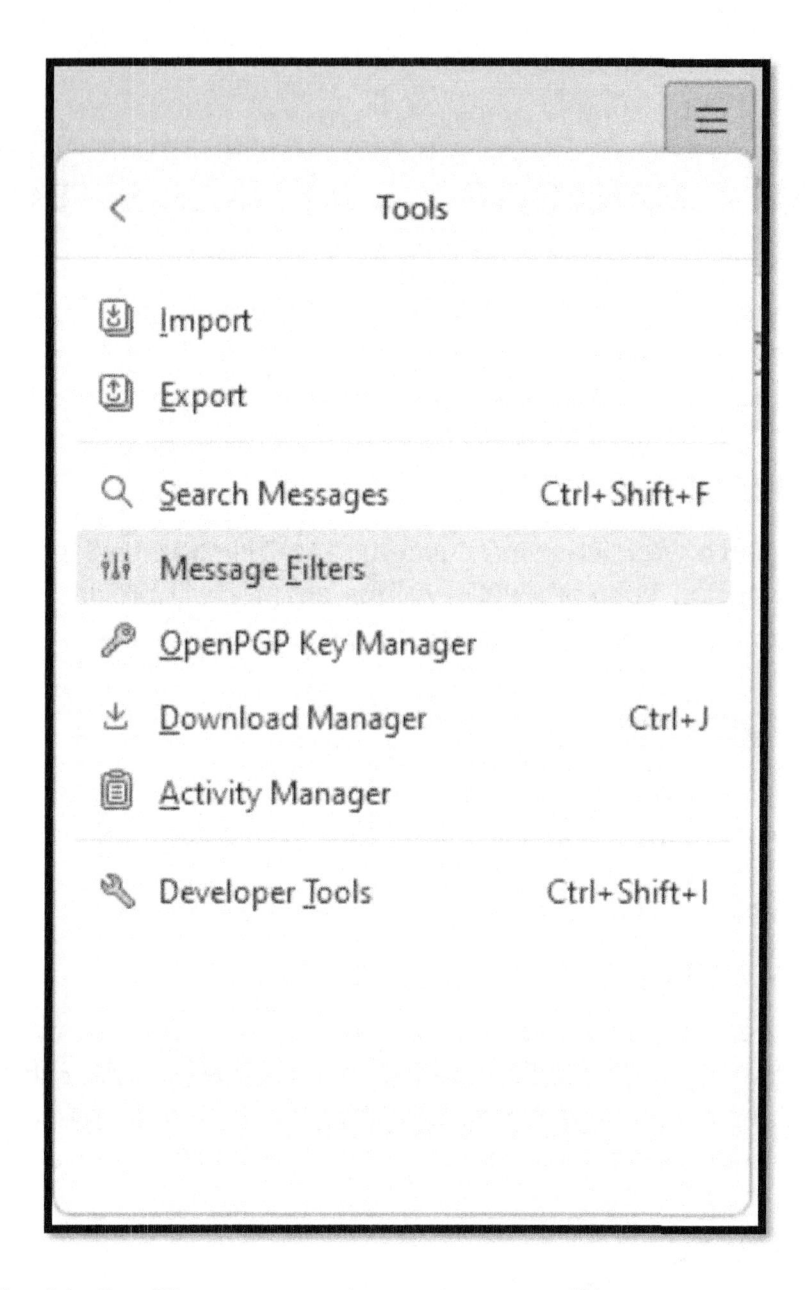

3. Click on "**New**" in the filter manager to create a new filter. create a new filter.
4. Enter a name for the new filter in the "**Filter rules**" dialog box in the "Filter rules" dialog box.
5. Select the conditions under which the filter is to be should be applied (e.g. "Subject", "Sender", "Recipient" etc.) and set the desired parameters.
6. Under "**Perfom these actions,** select the action that the filter should should perform when the conditions are met (e.g., "Move to," Copy to, "Mark as read", et c.).
7. Click on "**OK**" to save and activate the filter and activate it.

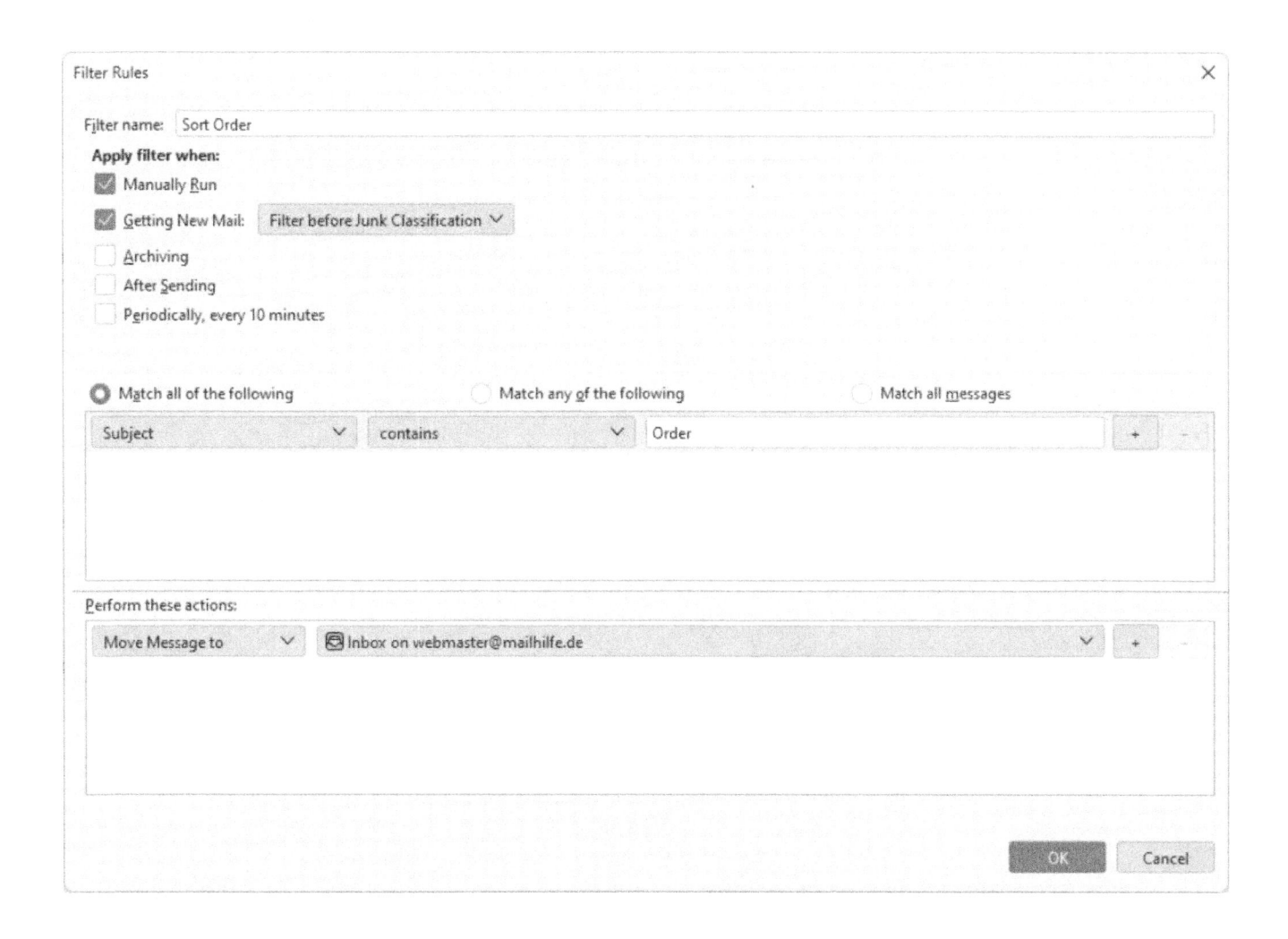

4.3.2 EDIT AND MANAGE FILTER RULES

In the Filter-Manager of Thunderbird Mail, you can manage, edit, and organize your filter rules:

1. To edit a filter, select the filter in the Filter Manager and click on "**Edit**." Change the criteria and actions as required and click "**OK**" to save your changes.
2. To delete a filter, select the filter in the filter manager and click on "**Delete**.".
3. To change the order of the filter rules, use the "**Move up**" and "**Move down**" buttons to move the selected filters up or down in the list. up or down in the list. The filters are applied in this order.

By using filters and rules in Thunderbird Mail, you can manage your emails more efficiently and keep your inbox without manual intervention.

4.3.3 EXAMPLE FOR THE CREATION OF A RULE

Using rules (also called filters) in Thunderbird can help you to manage your emails more efficiently. Below you will find a simple example of how to create a rule that moves all emails from a specific sender to a specific folder:

1. **Create a rule:** Open Thunderbird, click on the menu icon (three horizontal bars) in the top right corner of the window, and select "**Tools" > "Message Filters"**. Click on "**New**" to create a new filter.

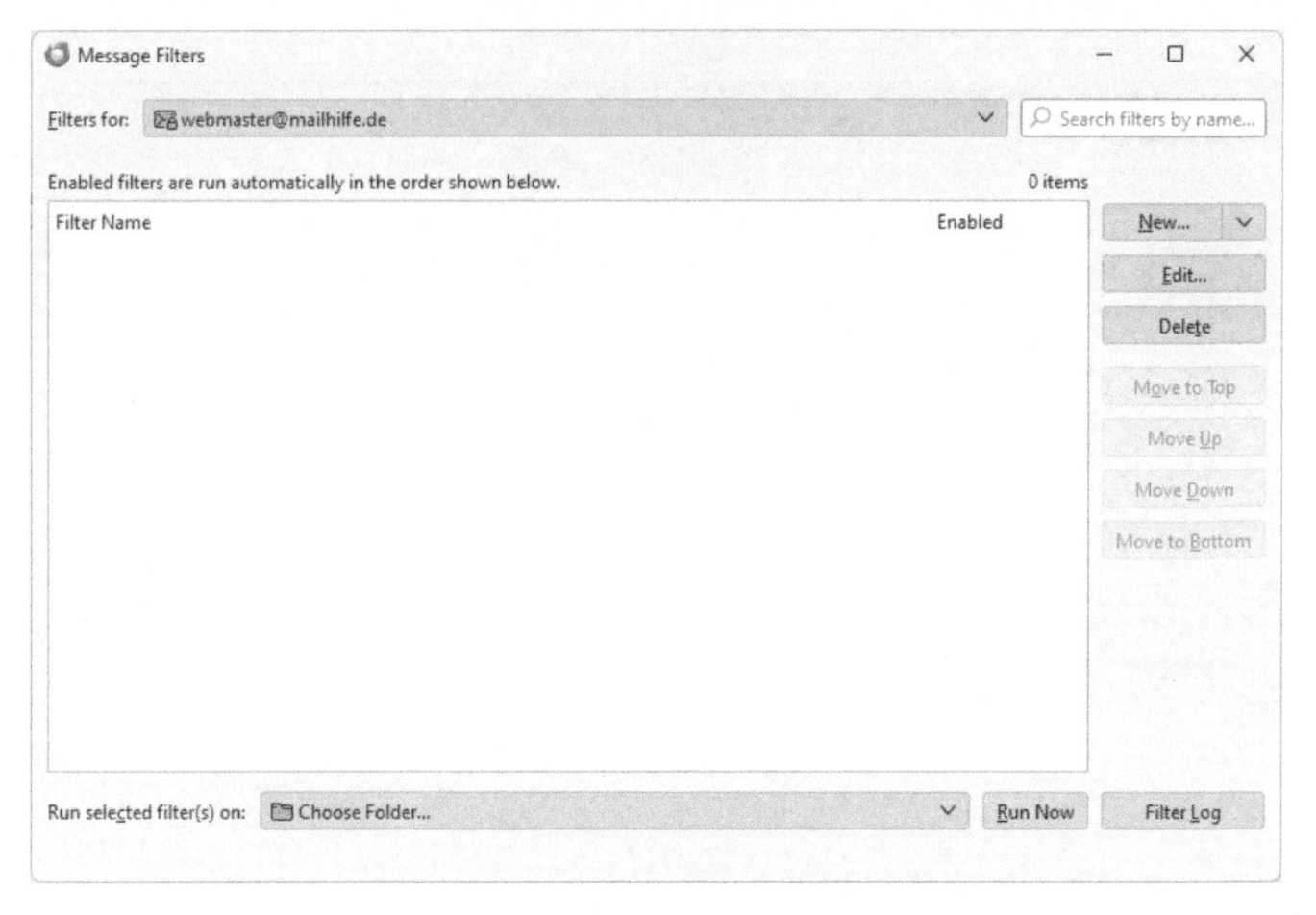

2. **Define the filter name and condition:** Assign a name for your filter, e.g. "*Emails from John*". In the Conditions section, specify that the "*From*" line contains "*JohnsEmail@example.com*".
3. Define action: In the "*Actions*" area, select "*Move message to.*" Then select the folder to which the message should be moved.
4. Test and save the filter: You can test the filter by clicking on "*Run Now*.".

Thunderbird now automatically moves all incoming emails from "*JohnsEmail@example.com*" to the selected folder. Create as many filters as you need to manage your emails efficiently.

4.4 ARCHIVING AND DATA BACKUP

It is crucial to implement effective archiving and data backup strategies in Thunderbird Mail to safeguard your valuable emails and data. These measures ensure the protection of your information and facilitate its restoration when needed.

4.4.1 E-MAIL ARCHIVING

Thunderbird Mail provides an archiving function that allows users to remove older emails from their inbox and save them in a separate archive folder. This feature allows users to maintain a clear and organized inbox while still having access to their archived emails.

To archive emails in Thunderbird, proceed as follows:

1. select the e-mail(s) you wish to archive.

2. right-click on the selected e-mail(s) and select "**Compact**" *from* the context menu, or simply press the" C key on your keyboard.

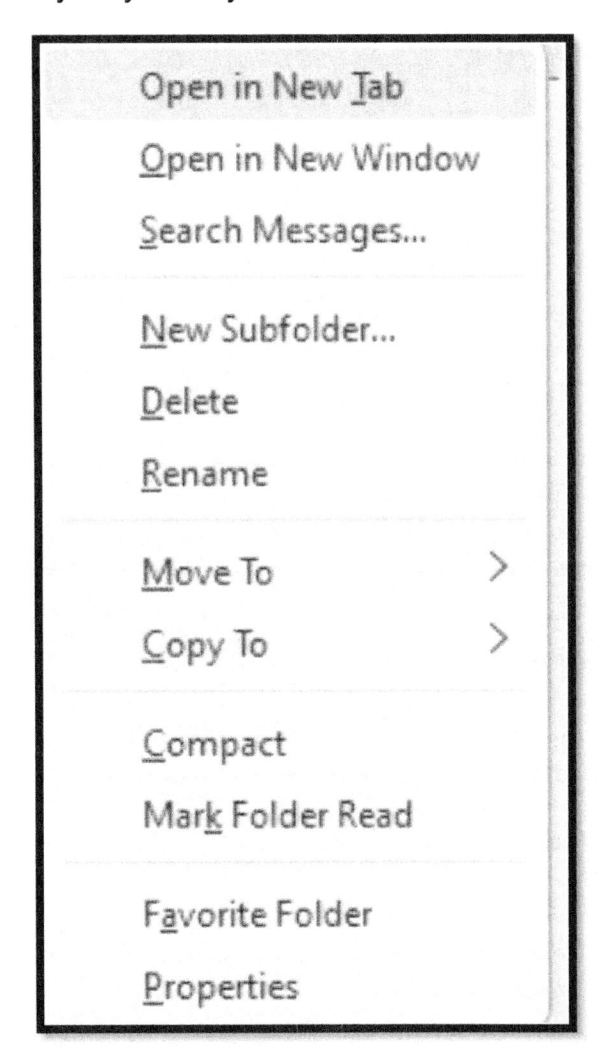

```
Open in New Tab
Open in New Window
Search Messages...

New Subfolder...
Delete
Rename

Move To                >
Copy To                >

Compact
Mark Folder Read

Favorite Folder
Properties
```

3. The selected emails are moved to the archive folder, which can be found by default under "**Local folders**" > "**Archive**".

You can adjust the archiving settings by navigating to "**Tools**" > "**Account settings**" > "**Copies & Folders**"> "**Message archive**". Here you can customize the folder structure for the archive and make further settings for archiving.

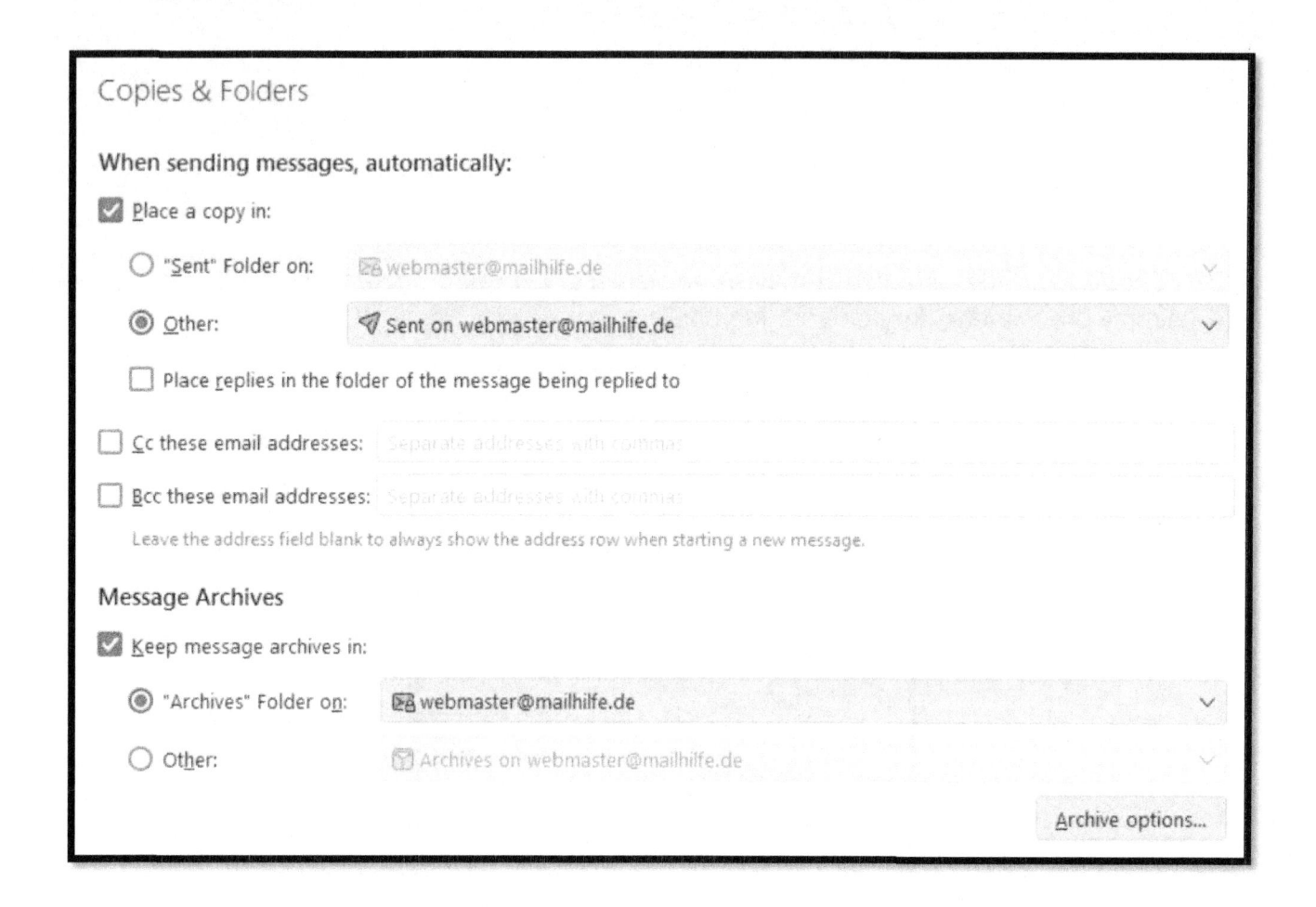

4.4.2 BACKING UP DATA

To back up your Thunderbird data, you should regularly create a backup of your Thunderbird profile, which contains all your emails, account settings, add-ons, and personal settings.

How to back up your Thunderbird profile

1. Close Thunderbird Mail.
2. Navigate to the Thunderbird profile folder on your computer. The storage location varies depending on the operating system.
    - **Windows**: C:\Users\ <your user name>\AppData\Roaming\Thunderbird\Profiles\
    - **macOS**: - /Library/Thunderbird/Profiles/
    - **Linux**: - /.thunderbird/.
3. Locate the profile folder (usually with a character string such as "***xxxxxx.default***") and copy the entire folder to a secure storage location, e.g., to an external hard disk, a USB stick, or a cloud storage service.
4. Keep the backup copy in a safe place so that you can restore it if necessary.

In the event of a data loss or computer crash, you can easily recover your Thunderbird data by copying the backed-up profile back to its original location or importing it into a new installation of Thunderbird.

By archiving and backing up regularly, you can ensure that your important emails and data are protected and can be easily recovered in the event of data loss or damage.

CHAPTER 5: ORGANIZING CONTACTS AND ADDRESS BOOK

Thunderbird Mail has an integrated address book where you can manage and organize your contacts. The Address Book makes it easy to add email addresses when composing messages and allows you to store additional information such as phone numbers, addresses, and notes.

5.1 OPENING AND MANAGING THE ADDRESS BOOK

To open the address book, click on the Address book button in the right-hand bar.

In the address book, you can manage your contacts in different folders, e.g., "Personal address book", "Collected addresses," and "Custom address books.".

5.2 ADDING AND EDITING CONTACTS

To add a new contact to the address book, proceed as follows:

1. Open the address book and select the address book in which you want to save the new contact.
2. Click on the "**New contact**" button or press **Ctrl + N** (Windows/Linux) or **Cmd + N** (macOS).

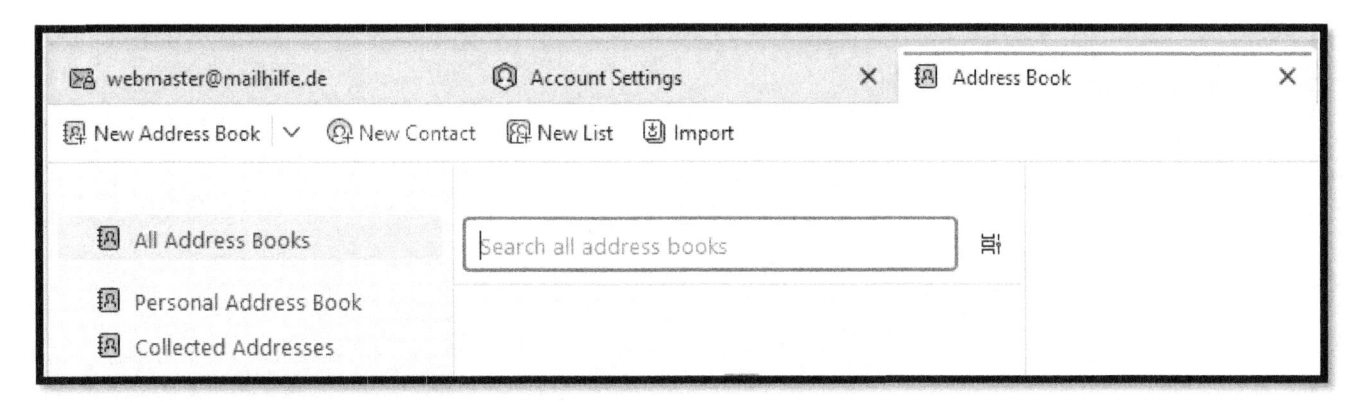

3. Enter the information for the new contact in the dialog box, e.g., name, email address, phone number, etc.
4. Click on "**Save**" to save the contact.

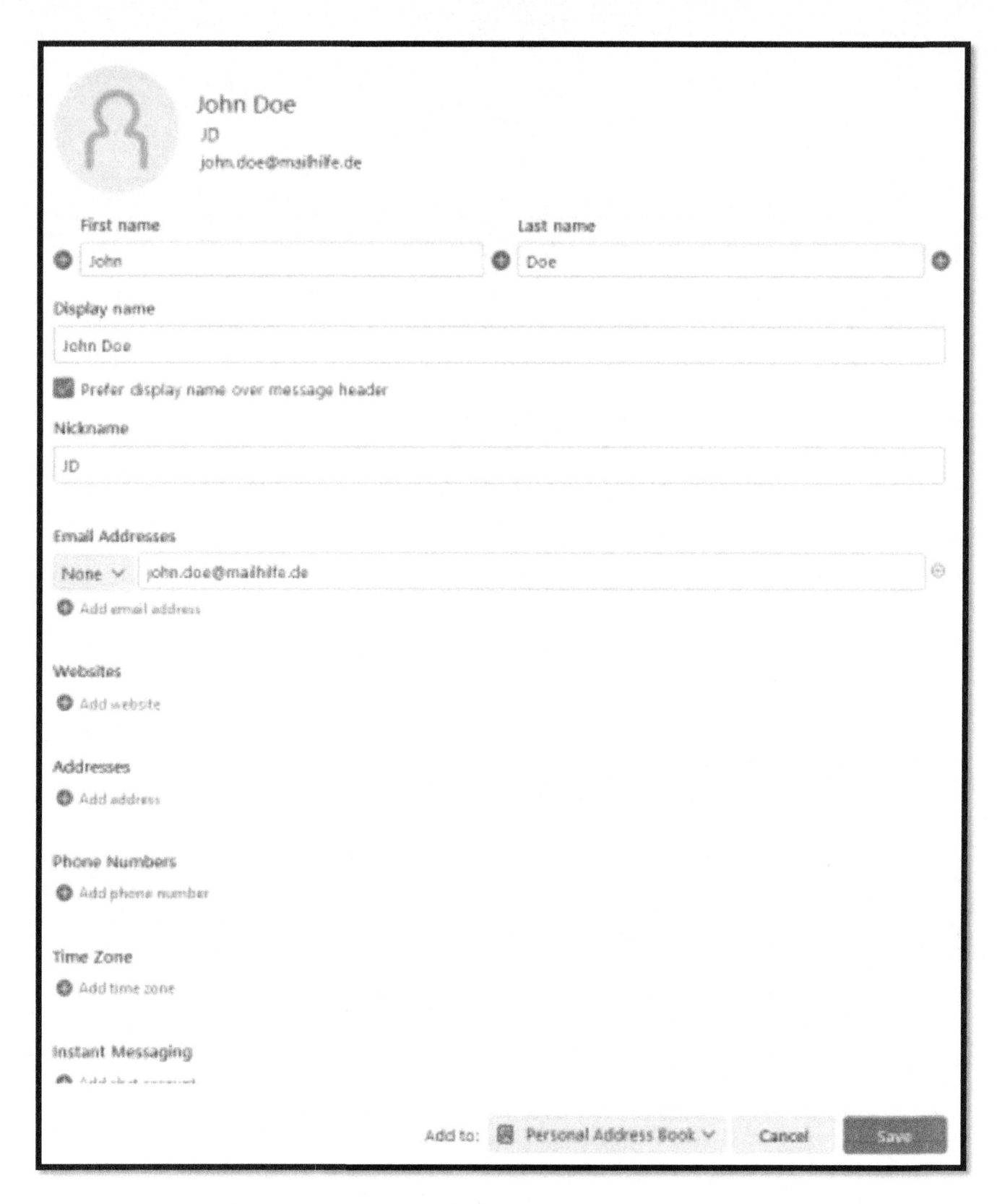

To edit an existing contact, double-click on the contact in the address book or select the contact and click on the "*Edit contact*" button. Change the contact information as required and click "*Save*" to save the changes.

5.4 CONTACTS IMPORT AND EXPORT

Thunderbird Mail enables the import and export of contacts in various formats, such as vCard

(VCF), LDIF, or CSV. This makes it easier to exchange data with other email clients or services.

5.4.1 TO IMPORT CONTACTS

1. Click on "**Address book**" and then "**Import**" from the menu.

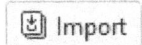

[Import]

2. In the "**Import**" dialog box, select the "**Address book**" option and click "**Next**".
3. Select the file format of the address book to be imported (e.g., vCard, LDIF, CSV) and click on "**Next**.".

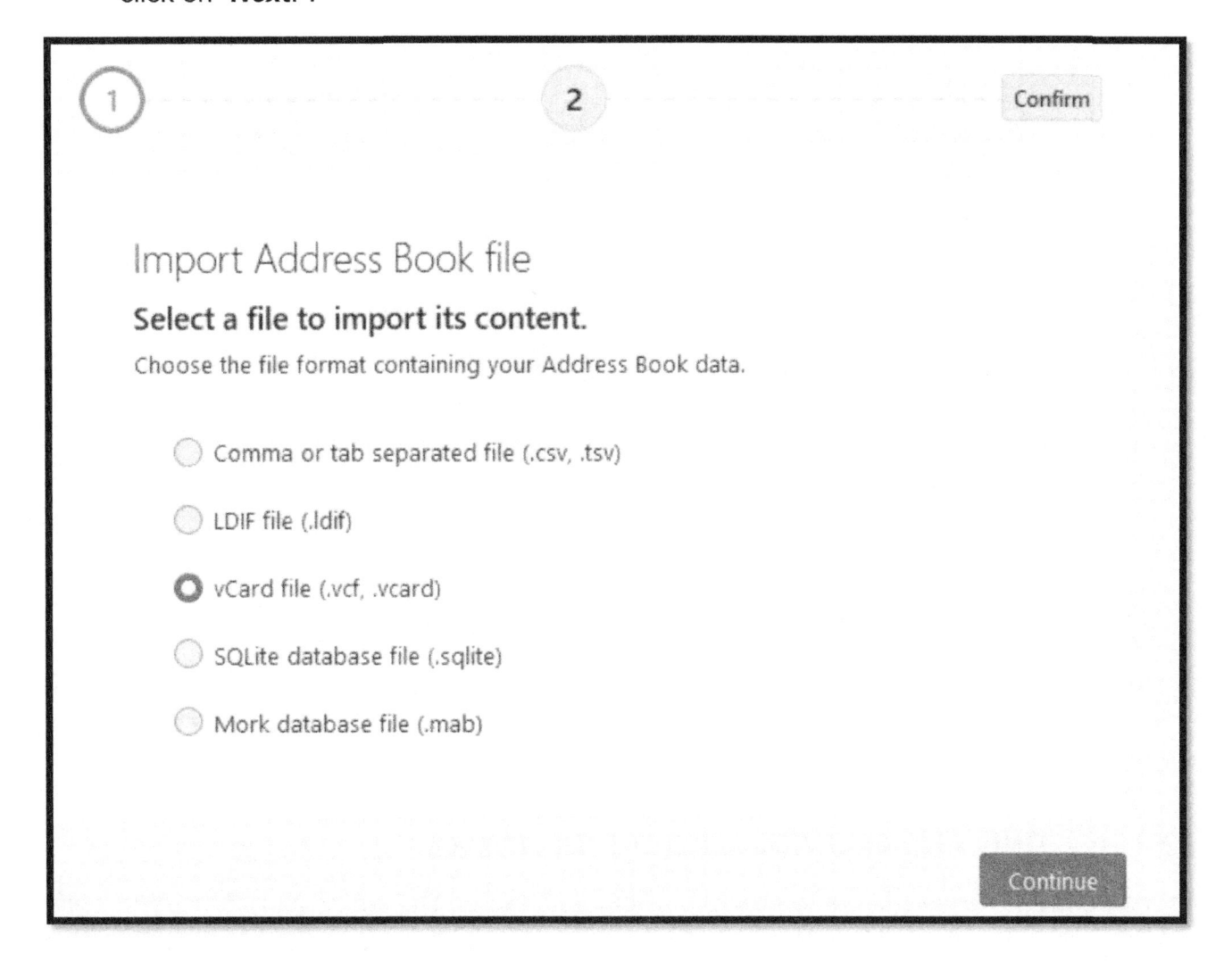

```
①                                    ②                                    Confirm

Import Address Book file
Select a file to import its content.
Choose the file format containing your Address Book data.

○ Comma or tab separated file (.csv, .tsv)
○ LDIF file (.ldif)
● vCard file (.vcf, .vcard)
○ SQLite database file (.sqlite)
○ Mork database file (.mab)

                                                                    Continue
```

4. Locate the file with the contacts to be imported and click on "**Open**".
5. Depending on the file format, you may be asked to assign fields or make additional settings. Follow the instructions on the screen and click on "**OK**" or "**Finish**" to complete the import.

5.4.2 TO EXPORT CONTACTS

1. Open the address book and select the address book you want to export.
2. Click on the menu icon (three horizontal bars) in the top right-hand corner of the window.
3. Select "**Extras**" and then "**Export**" from the menu.

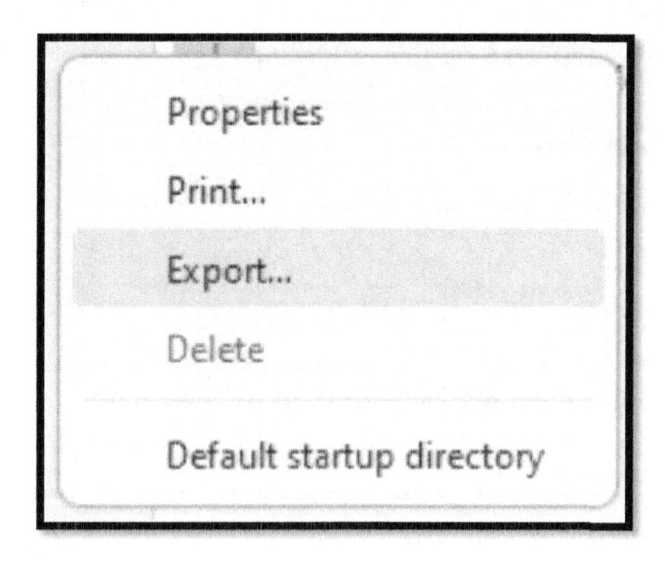

4. In the "***Export***" dialog box, select the desired file format for the exported address book (e.g., vCard, LDIF, CSV) and click on "**Save**".

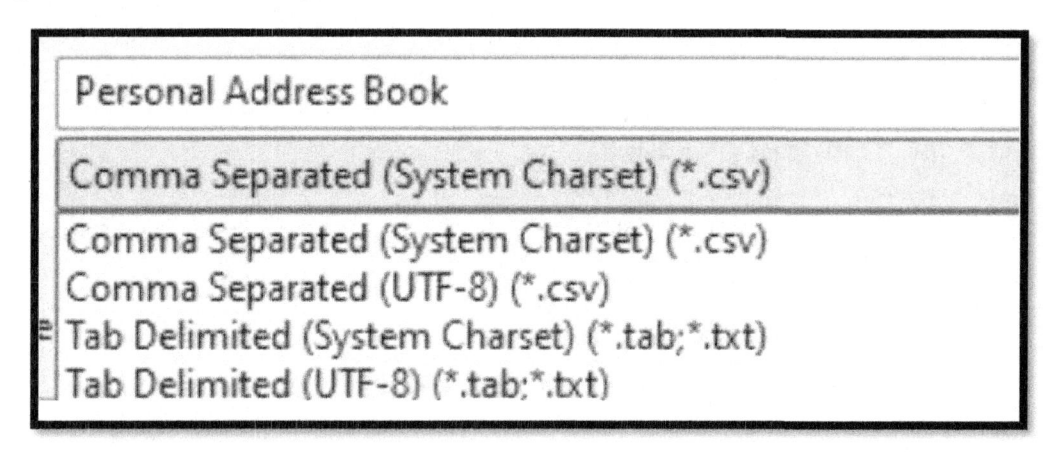

5. Enter a file name and a storage location for the exported file and click on "**Save**".

By importing and exporting contacts in Thunderbird Mail, you can easily transfer contacts between different e-mail between different email clients or services and ensure that your contact information is consistent and up-to-date.

5.5 CREATING AND MANAGINGADDRESS BOOKS

Thunderbird Mail allows users to create multiple address books, which can be used to better organize and manage their contacts. Custom address books can be created to group contacts by categories, projects, or other criteria, providing a more structured approach to contact management.

5.5.1 HOW TO CREATE A NEW ADDRESSBOOK IN THUNDERBIRD MAIL

1. Open the address book by clicking on the "Extras" menu icon and selecting "Address book.".
2. Select "***New address book***" from the menu.
3. Enter a name for the new address book in the "New address book" dialog box and click "***OK***."

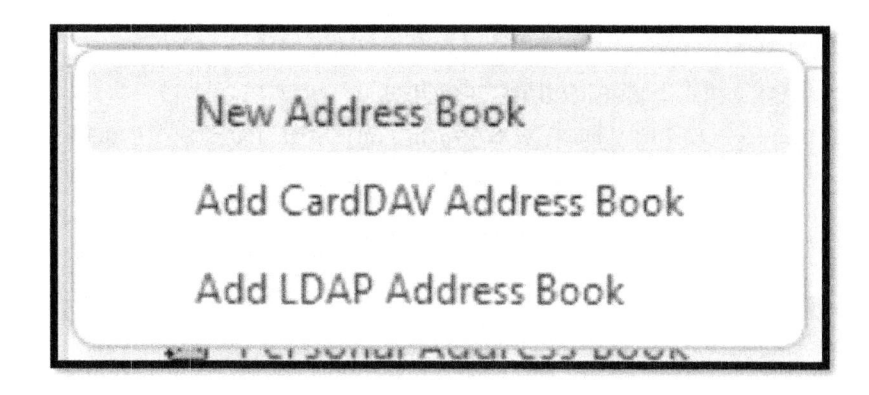

The newly created address book is displayed in the list of address books, and you can add or edit contacts or edit contacts as you are used to with the existing address books.

5.5.2 HOW TO MANAGE ADDRESS BOOKS

1. To move contacts between address books, simply drag the selected contacts from one address book to another.
2. To rename an address book, right-click on the address book in the list and select "**Properties**" from the context menu. Enter the new name and press the Enter key.
3. To delete an address book, right-click on the address book in the list and select "**Delete**" from the context menu. Please note that deleting an address book deletes all the contacts contained in it. are deleted.

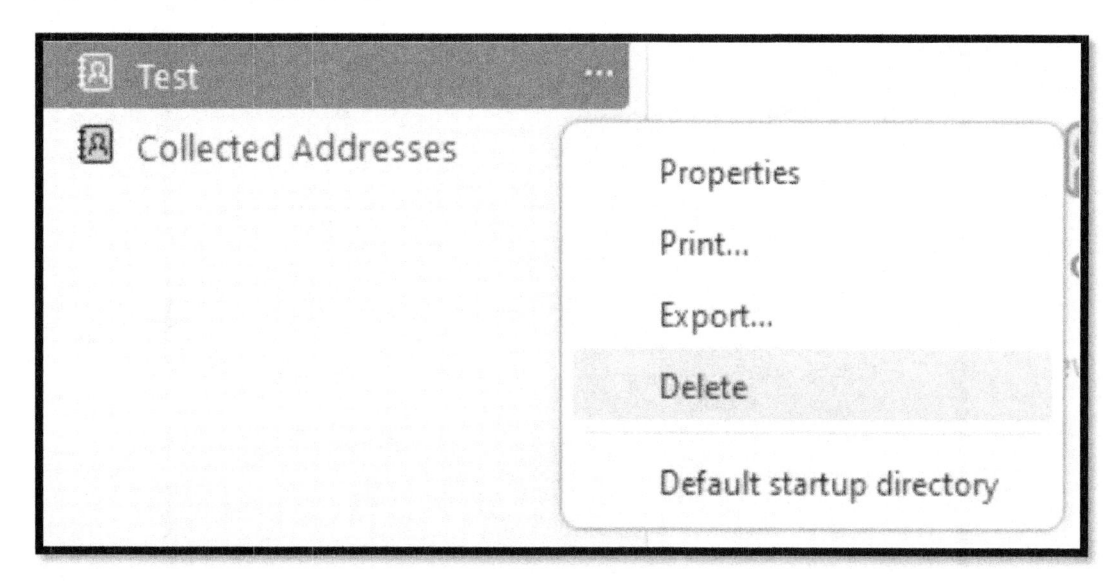

By creating and managing address books in Thunderbird Mail, you can streamline your contact management processes, enhance collaboration with colleagues, customers, and partners, and improve overall efficiency.

5.6 DISTRIBUTION LISTS AND GROUPS

In Thunderbird Mail, you can create distribution lists or groups to group several contacts and simplify and make it easier to send emails to multiple recipients. Distribution lists are useful if you frequently send them to the same group of people, e.g., team members, family, or friends.

5.6.1 HOW TO CREATE A DISTRIBUTION LIST IN THUNDERBIRD MAIL

1. Open the address book by selecting "***Address book***".
2. Select the address book in which you want to create the distribution list.
3. Click on the "***New List***" button or press ***Ctrl + L*** (Windows/Linux) or ***Cmd + L*** (macOS).

New List

4. Enter a name for the new distribution list in the "***New Mailing List***" dialog box.
5. To add contacts to the list, enter their e-mail address in the field and click on the button. press the Enter key. You can also drag existing contacts from your address book into the list.

6. Click on "***OK***" to save the distribution list.

To send an e-mail to the distribution list, simply write a new e-mail and enter the name of the distribution list in the "To," "Cc" or "Bcc" fields. Thunderbird Mail will automatically add all email addresses on the list as recipients.

CHAPTER 6: USING CALENDAR AND TASK MANAGEMENT

The "Lightning" add-on is already integrated in newer versions of Thunderbird and offers complete calendar and task management. With the integrated Lightning calendar, you can plan and manage appointments and tasks and synchronize them with other calendar services.

6.1 CREATING AND MANAGING CALENDARS

To create a new calendar in Thunderbird, proceed as follows:

1. Click on the calendar symbol on the left-hand side. At the bottom, click on the **New Calendar** button...

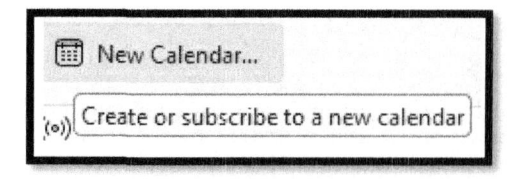

2. Select whether the new calendar should be saved locally or on a network server and click on "**Next**".

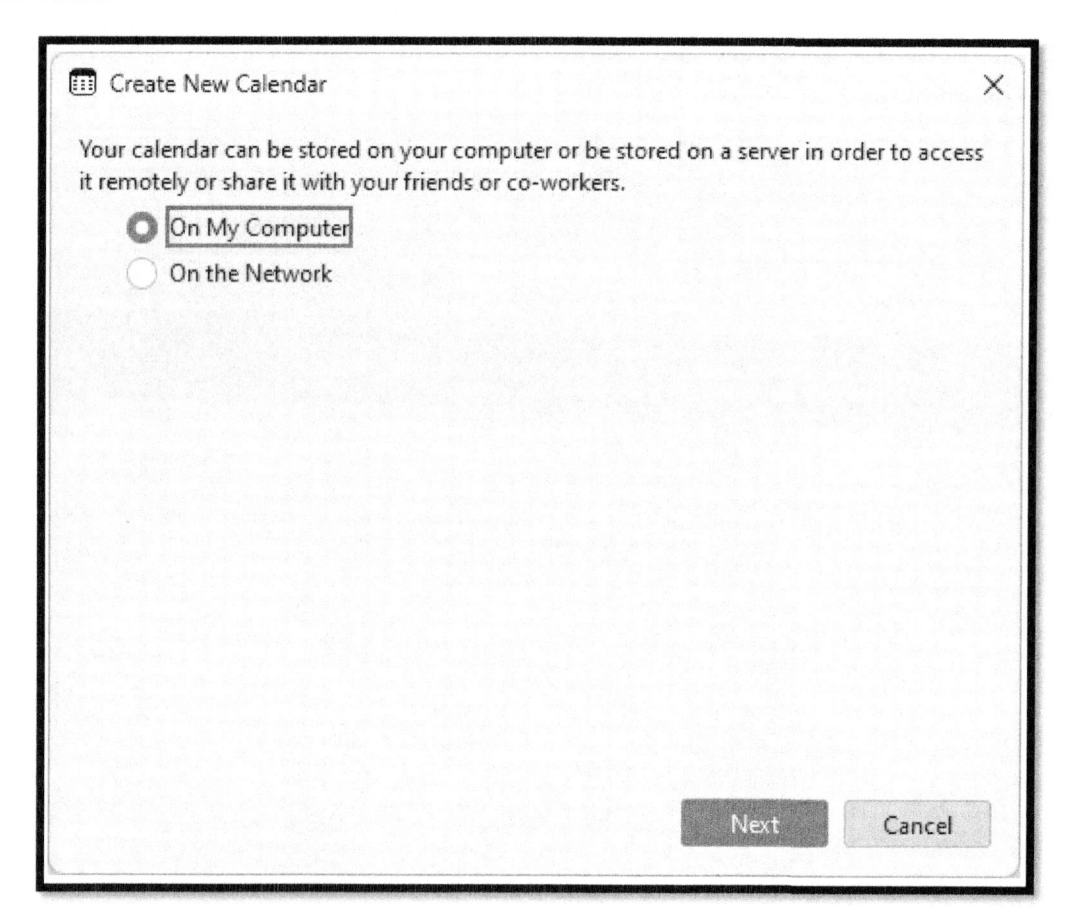

3. enter a name for the calendar, select a color and define further settings. Then click on "**Create Calendar**".

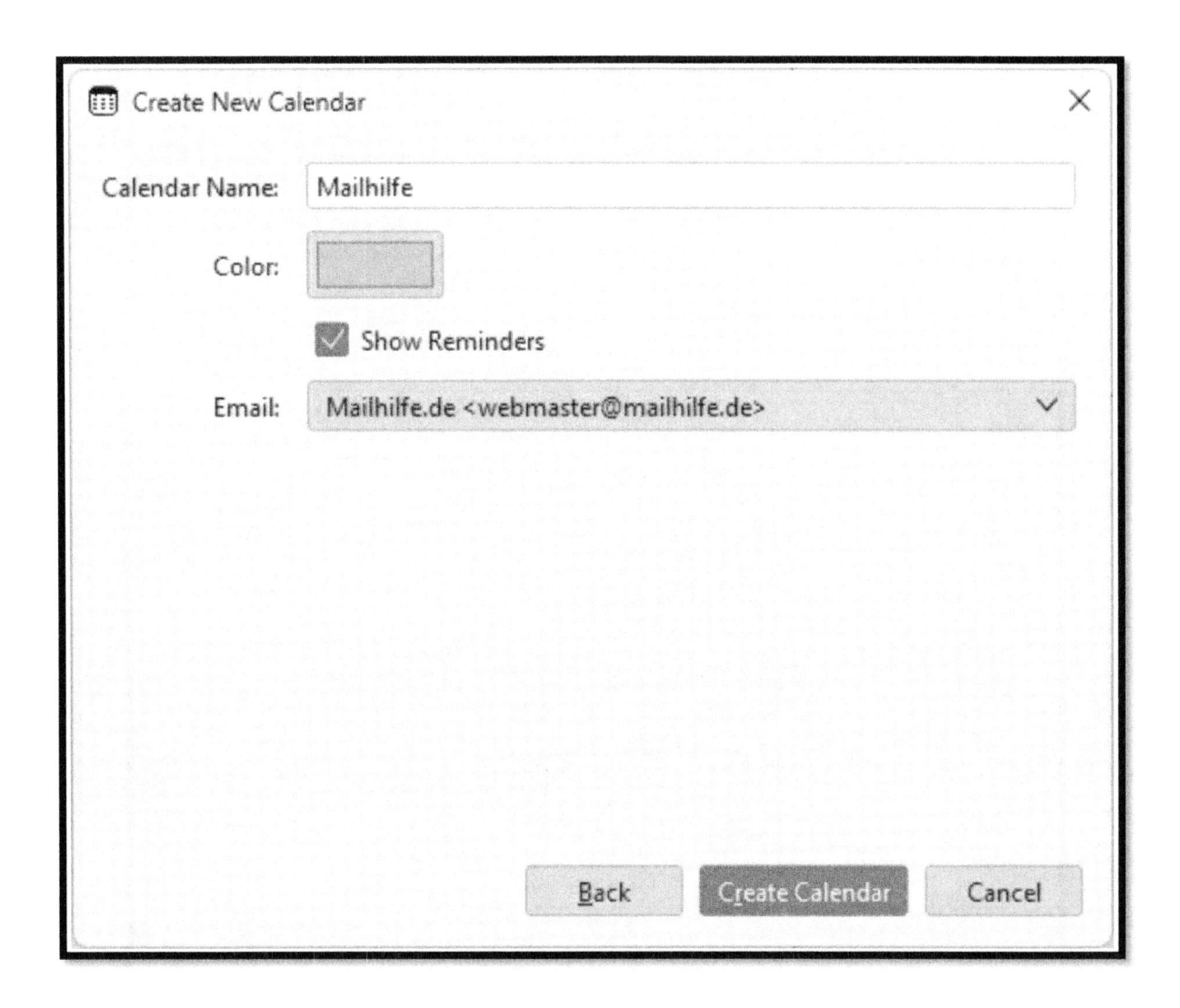

Once the calendar has been created, a new item appears in the menu overview: "**Events and Tasks**".

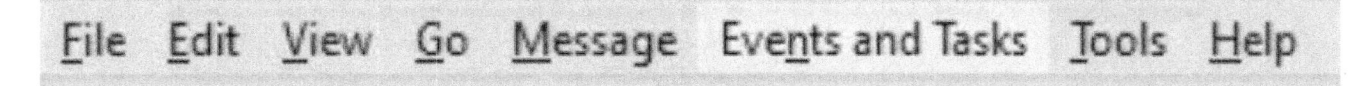

To create appointments and events, simply double-click on the desired date in the calendar or click on the "**New Event**" button .

Enter the required information for the event, e.g., title, date, time, location, and description, and click "**Save and close.**".

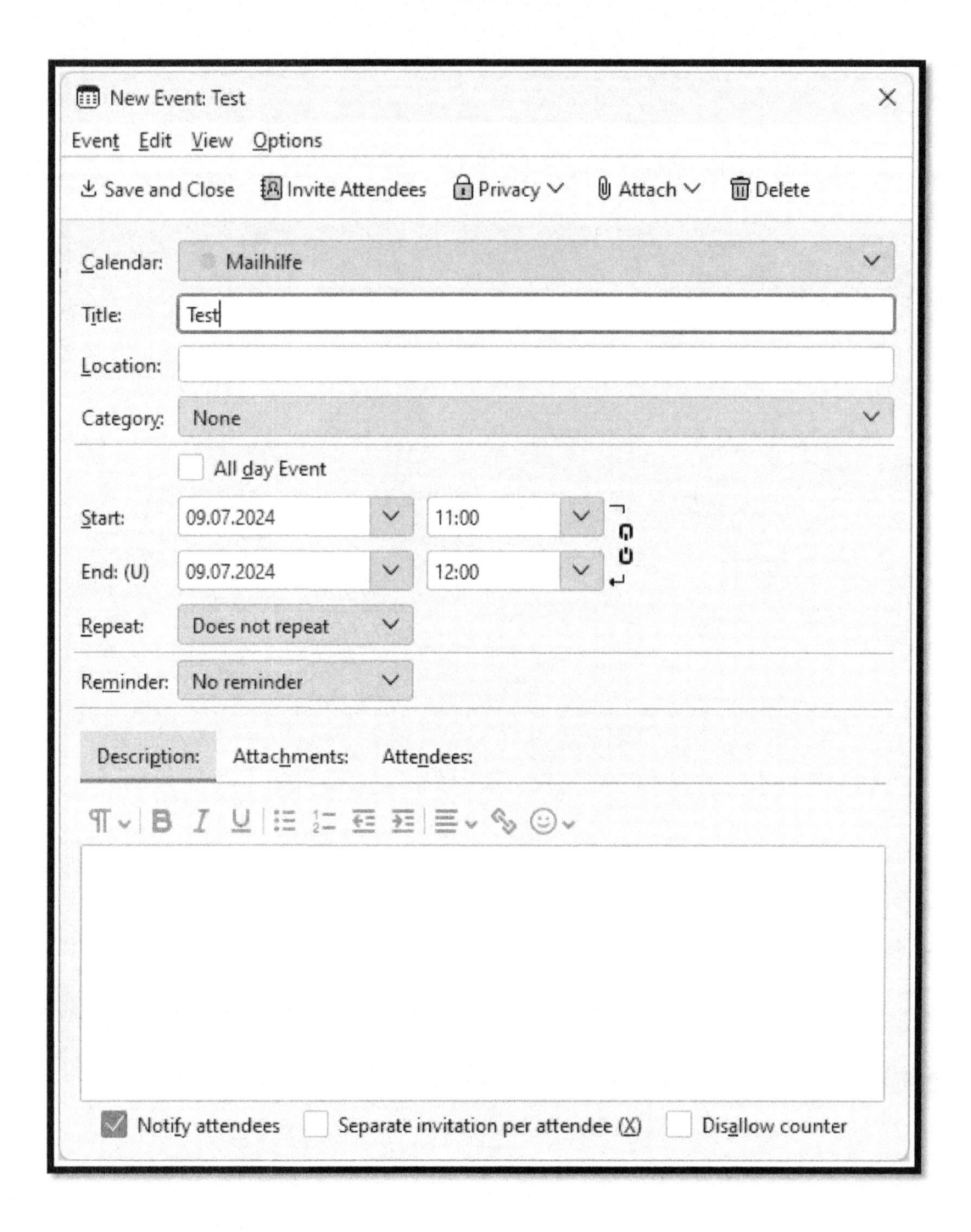

6.2 TASKS AND MEMORIES

Thunderbird offers integrated functions for managing tasks and reminders and reminders to help you stay organized and keep t rack of your upcoming tasks and appointments.

6.2.1 TASKS CREATE AND MANAGE

To create a new task in Thunderbird, proceed as follows:

1. In Thunderbird, click on the calendar icon in the top right-hand corner of the main window.
2. Switch to the "*Tasks*" tab" tab at the bottom of the calendar area.

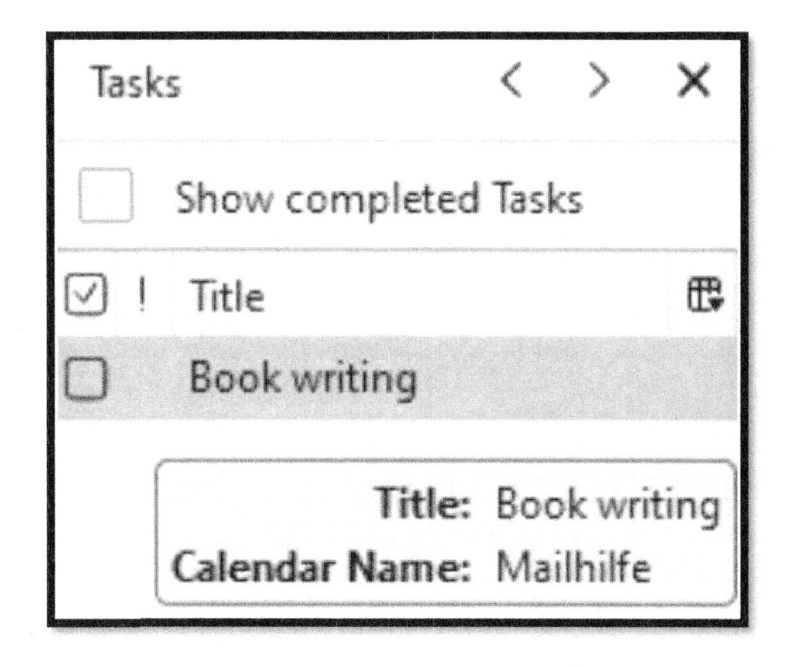

3. click on the "*Tasks*" button" button or press **Ctrl + Shift + T** (Windows/Linux) or **Cmd +Shift+ T** (macOS).
4. enter the required information for the task, e.g. title, date, priority and description. You can also set a reminder by activating the "*Reminder*" checkbox and selecting the date and time for the reminder. Click on "*Save and close*".

To manage tasks, you can mark them as completed by activating the checkbox next to the task or edit them by double-clicking on the task name.

Reminder messages for upcoming events and tasks are automatically displayed by Thunderbird. You can confirm the reminders by clicking on "**Done**" or postpone them to a later time by clicking on "**Postone Task**" and selecting a new time for the reminder.

6.3 SHARING A CALENDAR WITH OTHERS

Thunderbird allows you to share calendars with other people so they can see your appointments, events, and availability. To share a calendar in Thunderbird with other people, you can use CalDAV, an open standard for sharing calendar data. To set up a shared calendar

1. Select a CalDAV server: In order to use CalDAV, you will need a CalDAV server to host your calendar. Popular options include Google Calendar, iCloud, Next cloud, Zimbra, SOGo, or other CalDAV-enabled servers. Set up an account with one of these providers or use your existing account.
2. Set up the CalDAV calendar in Thunderbird: Open Thunderbird and click on the calendar icon in the top right-hand corner of the main window to go to the calendar area.
3. Right-click on the empty area on the left under "**Calendar**" and select "**New calendar**...".

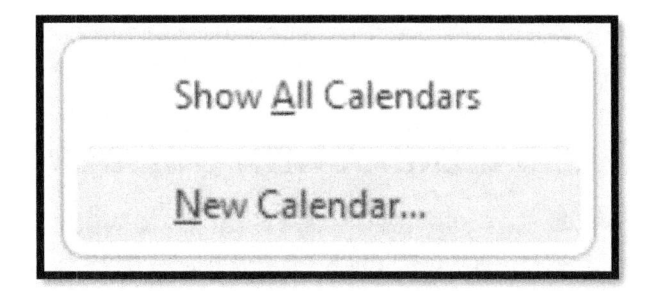

4. Select "**In the network**" in the setup wizard and click on "**Next**".

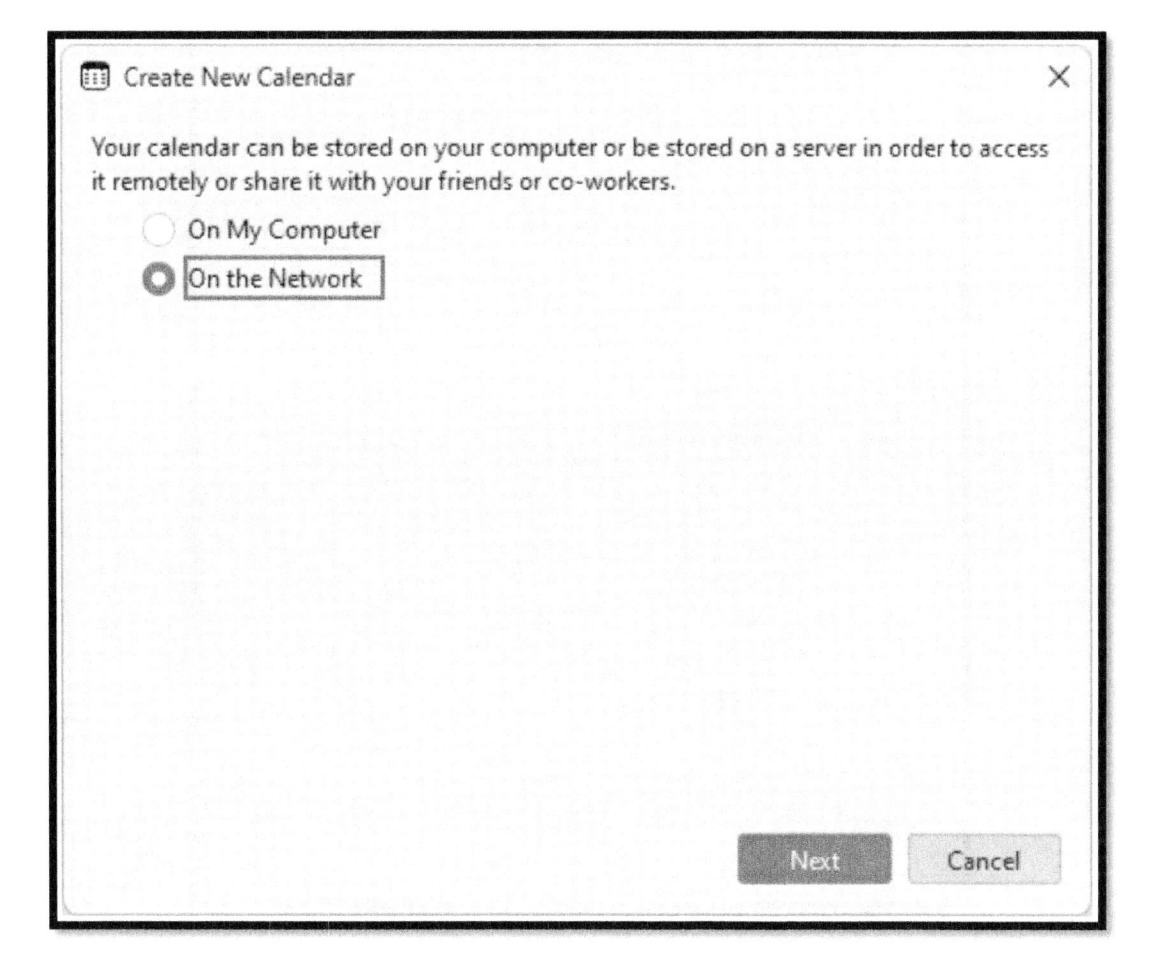

5. Select the calendar you want to set up in Thunderbird and click "***Next***". Give the calendar a name and choose a color to highlight it in the calendar area. Click on "***Next***." For Google Calendar, you can find the required URLs in the Google Calendar settings. For other providers, look for instructions on how to find or create the CalDAV-URL can be found or created.
6. Enter your user name and password for the CalDAV server and click "Next." -server and click on "***Next"*** and then on "***Finish***".

Now you can manage your calendar in Thunderbird, and all changes are automatically synchronized with the CalDAV-server automatically. To share your calendar with other people, give them the CalDAV URL and the required credentials. They can then add and view your calendar in their favorite calendar application if it supports CalDAV.

Note: The steps for sharing a calendar may vary depending on the CalDAV server used. It is therefore recommended that you follow your provider's specific instructions to ensure that your calendar is shared correctly.

6.3.1 SHARING GOOGLE CALENDAR WITH THUNDERBIRD

1. Retrieve the URL of the Google calendar; Sign in to your Google account and open Google Calendar. In the left sidebar, click on the three dots next to the calendar you want to share,

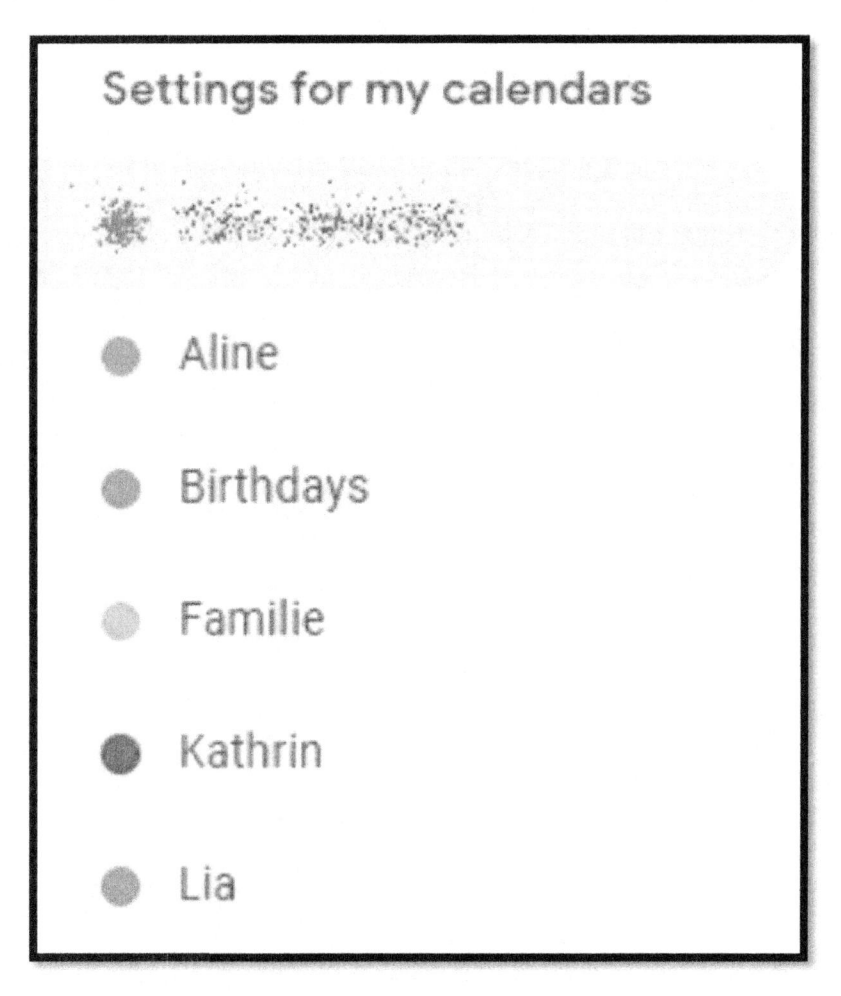

Settings for my calendars

- Aline
- Birthdays
- Familie
- Kathrin
- Lia

and select "***Settings and sharing.***"

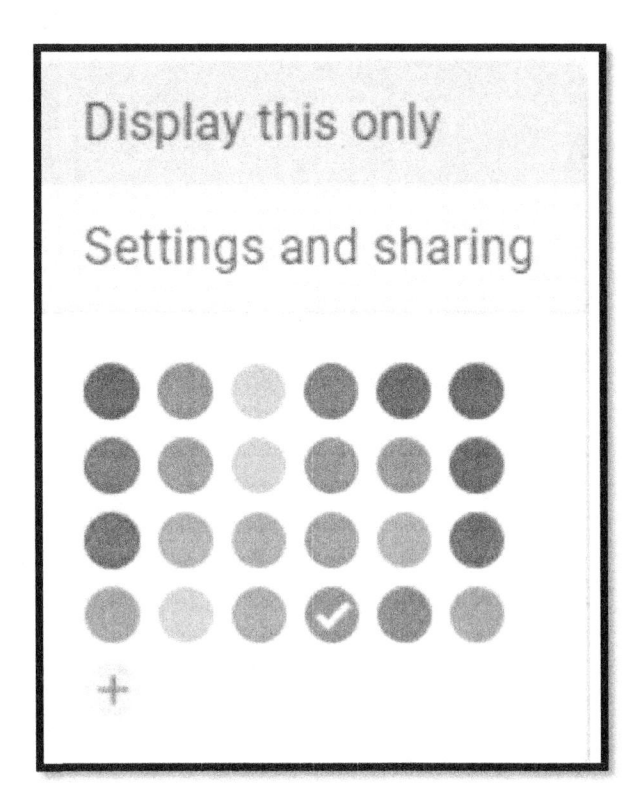

In the calendar settings, scroll down to the "*Integrate calendar*" section and copy the "CalDAV-address".

2. Open Thunderbird and click on the calendar icon in the top right corner of the main window to go to the calendar area. Right-click on the empty area on the left under "*Calendar*" and select "*New calendar...*".
3. Select "*In the network*" in the setup wizard and click on "*Next*".

4. Enter the e-mail address linked to your Google account and paste the address from your Google calendar. Then click on "*Search calendar.*".

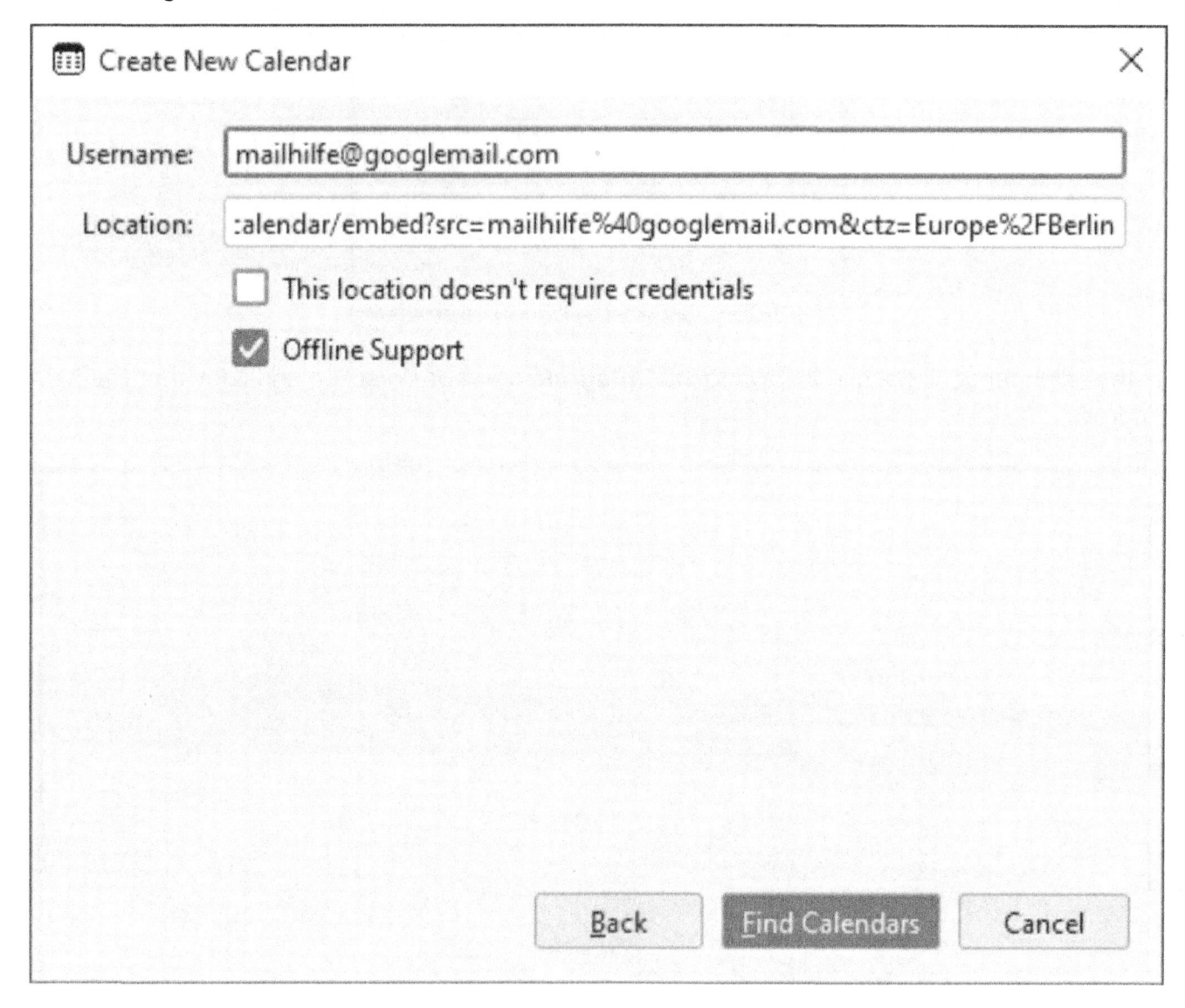

```
Create New Calendar                                              X

Username:  mailhilfe@googlemail.com

Location:  :alendar/embed?src=mailhilfe%40googlemail.com&ctz=Europe%2FBerlin

           ☐ This location doesn't require credentials
           ☑ Offline Support




                                      Back    Find Calendars    Cancel
```

5. a browser window will open. You must then enter your access data here.

Mit Google-Konto anmelden
@googlemail.com
Passwort eingeben
Anmeldung
Angemeldet bleiben
Passwort vergessen?

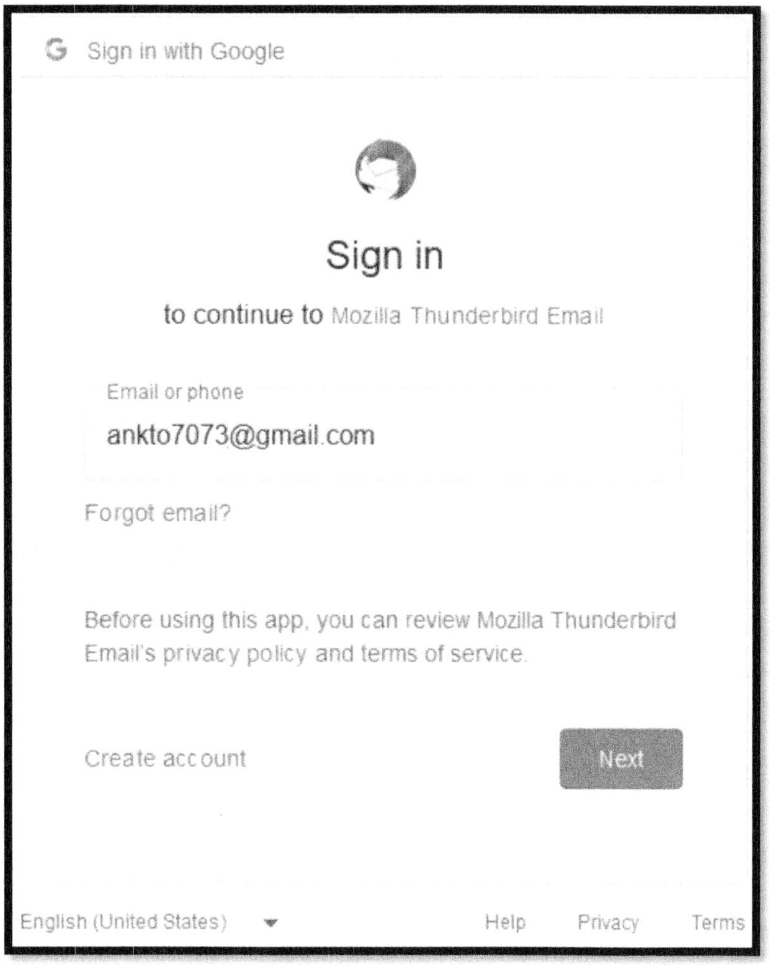
Sign in with Google
Sign in
to continue to Mozilla Thunderbird Email
Email or phone
ankto7073@gmail.com
Forgot email?
Before using this app, you can review Mozilla Thunderbird Email's privacy policy and terms of service.
Create account
Next
English (United States)
Help
Privacy
Terms

If everything has worked, a new window should appear "Mozilla Thunderbird Email needs access to your Google account", here click on "***Allow***".

Google
Mozilla Thunderbird Email benötigt Zugriff auf Ihr Google-Konto
mailhilfe@googlemail.com
Dadurch erhält Mozilla Thunderbird Email diese Berechtigungen:
Alle Kalender, die über Google Kalender verfügbar sind, aufrufen, bearbeiten, freigeben und endgültig löschen
Durch Klicken auf "Zulassen" gewähren Sie dieser App und Google gemäß der jeweiligen Datenschutzerklärung Zugriff auf Ihre Daten. Sie können diese und andere Kontoberechtigungen jederzeit ändern.
Ablehnen
Zulassen

6. If you manage several calendars in Google Calendar, you must select a corresponding calendar.

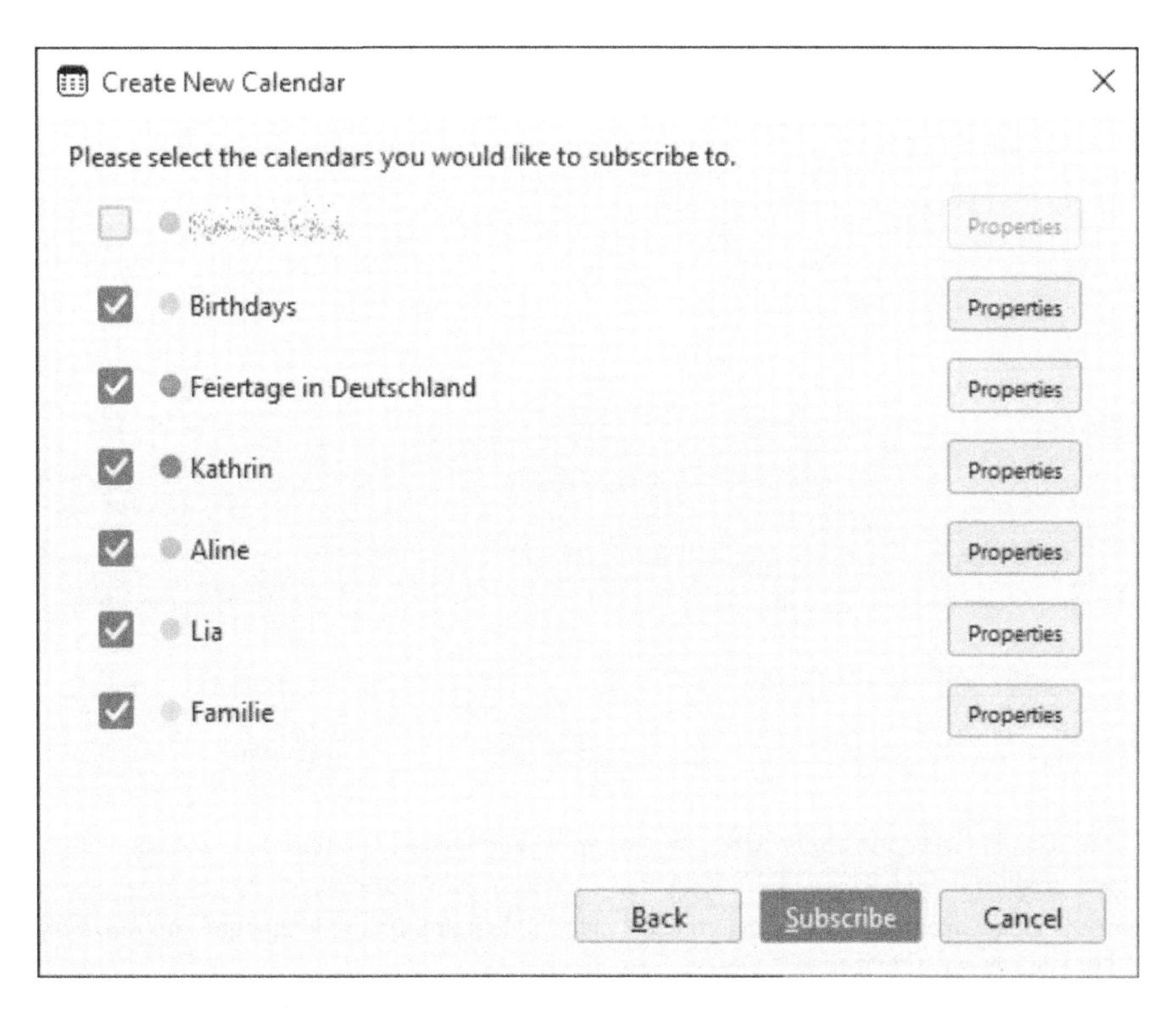

7. you can define the behavior of the calendar in the "**Properties**.".

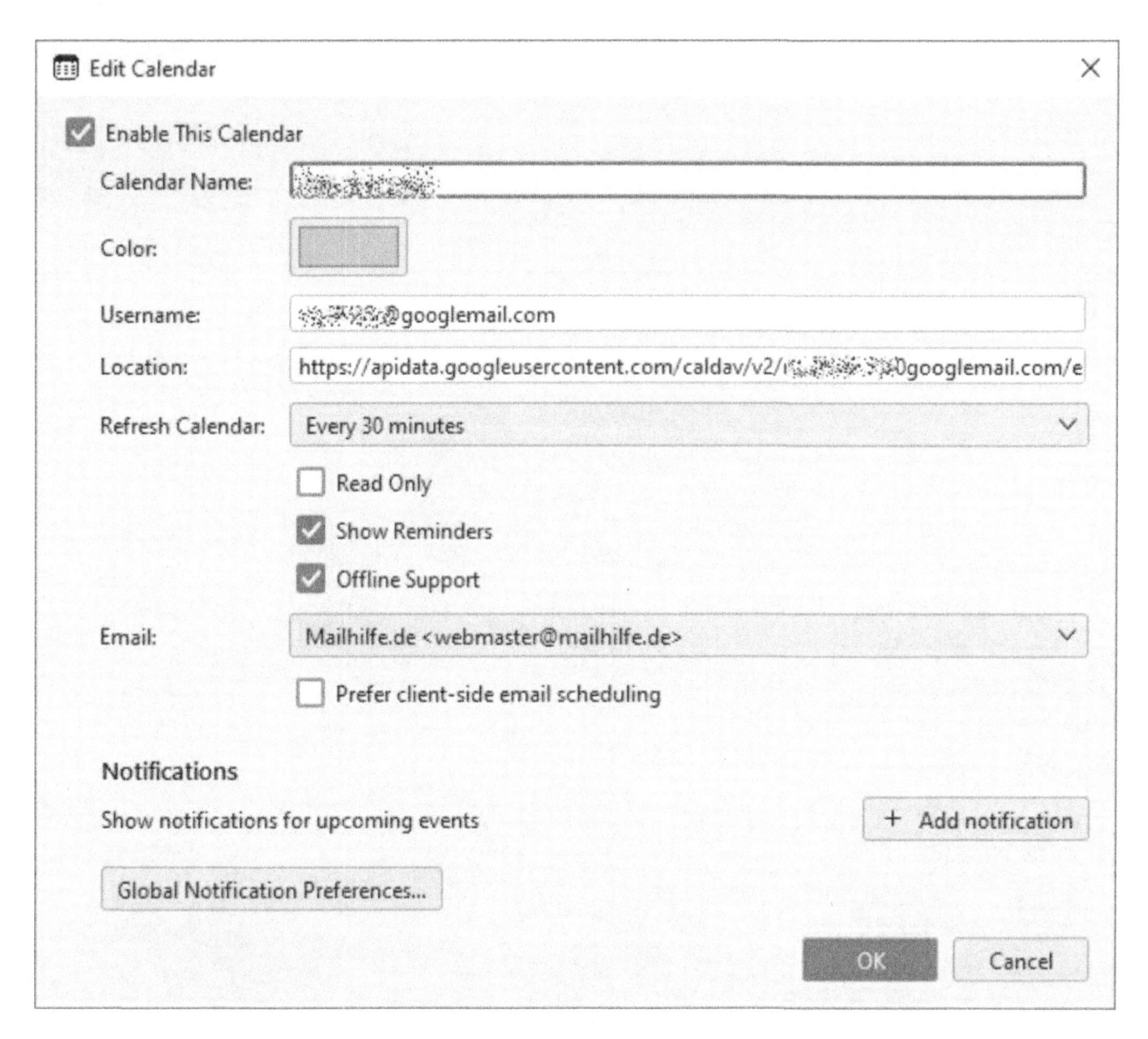

8. Confirm everything with "**OK**" and then with "**Subscribe**" The new calendar should now be played on the left-hand side.

Your Google Calendar is now synchronized with Thunderbird, and any changes you make are automatically synchronized with Google Calendar.

To share your Google Calendar with other people, go back to the calendar settings in the Google Calendar web app (step 1), scroll to the "**Sharing settings**" section, and enter the email addresses of the people you want to share your calendar with. You can also set different per-mission levels, e.g., whether the person can only view the calendar or also edit it. Invited persons will receive an email with an invitation to view or edit the calendar, depending on the permissions set.

CHAPTER 7: EXPLORING ADVANCED FEATURES

This chapter covers advanced features of Thunderbird that can help you further optimize your email and organization capabilities. These features include

7.1 **Add-ons and extensions:** Learn how to install, manage, and uninstall add-ons and extensions to extend the functionality of Thunderbird. This includes additional security features, automated processes, email organization tools, and much more.

7.2 **Message templates:** Create and use templates for recurring messages to save time and effort when you frequently send similar emails.

7.3 **Signature**: Set up a personalized email signature that is automatically attached to every message you send. Learn how to create and manage multiple signatures for different accounts or situations.

7.4 **RSS feeds and newsgroups:** Subscribe to and manage RSS feeds from news sites, blogs, and other online sources directly in Thunderbird to stay up to date.

7.5 **Email rules and filters** Create user-defined rules and filters to automatically sort, mark, forward, or delete incoming and outgoing messages. Learn how to create and manage filters for different situations and requirements.

7.6 **Chat integration**: Integrate instant messaging and chat services such as Google Talk, IRC, or XMPP directly into Thunderbird to manage all your communication channels in one place.

These advanced features allow you to customize Thunderbird to your needs and increase your productivity in email communication and organization. By learning and using these features, you can use Thunderbird more effectively and efficiently.

7.1 ADD-ONS AND EXTENSIONS

Add-ons and extensions are additional software components that can be installed in Thunderbird to extend its functionality and improve its user-friendliness. Add-ons allow you to customize Thunderbird to your individual needs and preferences. In this section, you will learn how to find, install, manage, and uninstall add-ons.

7.1.1 HOW TO FIND ADDONS

Thunderbird has an integrated addon manager that provides access to a variety of add-ons. To open the Add-ons Manager, click on the menu icon (three horizontal bars) in the top right corner of the Thunderbird window and select "***Add-ons and Themes > Extensions.***" In the Add-ons Manager, you can search for specific add-ons in the search field or browse different categories to find add-ons that meet your needs.

Alternately, you can also visit the official Thunderbird add-ons website (https://addons.thunderbird.net or our Thunderbird extensions collection (https://www.mailhilfe.de/downloads/thunderbird-tools to search for and download add-ons.

7.1.2 INSTALLING ADD-ONS

To install an add-on in Thunderbird, proceed as follows:

1. open the Add-on Manager as described above.
2. Search for the desired add-on and click on the "**Add to Thunderbird**" button.
3. A dialog appears in which you must confirm the installation. Read the authorizations required by the add-on and click on "**Install add-on**" if you agree.
4. Some add-ons may require a restart of Thunderbird to complete the installation. If this is the case, save all open work and click on "**Restart now**".

7.1.3 MANAGING ADD-ONS

After installation, you can manage your add-ons in the Addons Manager. There you can view information about each installed add-on, including the version, the author, and a description of the functions. You can also activate or deactivate add-ons or change their settings. To change the settings of an add-on, click on the "**Settings**" or "**Options**" button next to the add-on.

7.1.4 UNINSTALLING ADD-ONS

If you no longer need an add-on or it is causing problems, you can uninstall it in the Add-on Manager. To do this, proceed as follows:

1. Open the Add-on Manager as described above.
2. Find the add-on you want to remove and click on the "**Remove**" button.

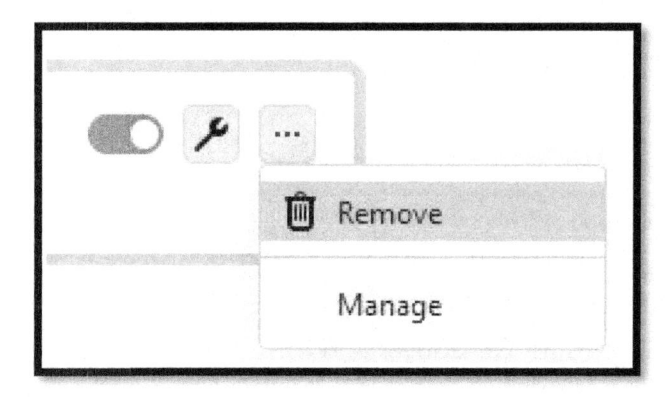

3. Some add-ons may require a restart of Thunderbird to complete the uninstallation. If this is the case, save all open documents and click on "**Restart now.**".

Removing an add-on deletes all associated data and settings from Thunderbird. Make sure that you back up all important information before you uninstall an add-on.

7.1.5 ADD-ON CATEGORIES AND EXAMPLES

There are many different categories of add-ons that provide a variety of features and enhancements for Thunderbird. Some of the most common add-on categories are

- **Security and data protection:** Add-ons that offer additional security features such as encryption, anti-spam tools, and advanced authentication options.
- **Productivity**: Add-ons that help you to better organize and manage your emails and tasks better organized and managed, e.g., calendar extensions, task managers, and automatic reply tools.
- **User interface and customization:** add-ons that change the appearance of Thunderbird or extend the user interface with new functions, e.g., themes, toolbar customizations, and extended menu options.
- **Communication**: Add-ons that offer additional communication functions such as chat integration, VoIP support, or extended e-mail notifications.
- **Webservice integration:** Add-ons that connect Thunderbird with other online services and applications such as cloud storage, social networks, or CRM systems.

Some examples of popular add-ons are

- **Enigmail** A plug in that enables PGP-encryption and signing in Thunderbird.
- **Card Book:** A powerful address book add-on that improves the management of contacts and distribution lists. improved.
- **Quick Folders** An add-on that simplifies and speeds up the management of email folders by providing customized shortcuts and actions for frequently used folders.

Overall, add-ons and extensions allow you to customize Thunderbird to your needs and increase productivity through additional features and improvements. By searching for and installing add-ons that are relevant to your way of working and needs, you can get the most out of Thunderbird.

7.2 MESSAGE TEMPLATES

Message templates are pre-formatted email texts that you can use to quickly create and send recurring or similar emails. Instead of typing the same text every time, templates can save you time and effort and ensure that your emails look consistent and professional. In this section, you will learn how to create, use, and manage email templates in Thunderbird.

7.2.1 CREATE TEMPLATES

To create a message template in Thunderbird, proceed as follows:

1. Open Thunderbird and click on **"Compose" to open** a new e-mail window.
2. Enter the desired text and formatting for your template. You can also add subject, attachments, recipients, and CC/BCC fields if you want this information to be saved in the template.

3. Click on "*Save as template*" in the "*File" -> "Save as*" menu. Your template will now be saved in the "Templates" folder, which can be found in the Thunderbird folder list under "Local folders.".

7.2.2 USING TEMPLATES

To use a saved template for a new e-mail, proceed as follows:

1. Right-click on the "*Templates*" folder under "*Local folders"* in the Thunderbird folder list and select "*New subfolder*.".
2. Enter a name for the new subfolder and click on "*Create folder."*.

3. Drag the desired template from the "***Templates***" folder into the newly created subfolder.
4. Double-click on the template in the subfolder to open a new email with the content of the template. Edit the email as required and send it as usual.

7.2.3 MANAGE TEMPLATES

Templates can be managed in Thunderbird like normal emails. You can move, copy, delete or rename them by right-clicking on the template in the folder list and selecting the appropriate option from the context menu. To edit a template, double-click on the template to open it in the editing window, make the desired changes, and then click on "***Save as template***" in the "***File***"->"***Save as***" menu to save the updated version.

7.2.4 TIPS FOR THE EFFECTIVEUSE OF TEMPLATES

- Create templates for frequently used email types, such as requests, replies, confirmations, or complaints, to save time when creating emails.

- Use placeholders to mark areas in the template that need to be customized before sending. For example, you can use "[recipient name]" or "[date]" as placeholders for personalized information.

- Organize your templates in subfolders within the template folder to make them easier to find and access. You can organize subfolders by email type, purpose, or department.

- Create templates with different formatting and styles to meet the requirements of different communication situations. For example, you can create formal templates for business communication and informal templates for internal use.

- Share useful templates with colleagues or team members by sending them by email or saving them in a shared network folder. This way, all team members can benefit from the created templates and ensure consistent communication within the organization.

- Review your templates regularly to ensure they are up-to-date and relevant. Update outdated information, correct typos, and adjust the formatting if necessary.

Overall, message templates in Thunderbird are an effective tool to improve the efficiency and consistency of your email communications. By creating and using templates that meet your specific needs, you can save time, improve the quality of your emails, and ensure that your communication is professional and consistent.

7.3 SIGNATURE

The email signature is an important part of business communication. It provides the recipient with important contact details and information about the sender and contributes to a uniform and professional appearance. In Thunderbird, you can create one or more signatures and attach them to your emails automatically or manually.

7.3.1 CREATE SIGNATURE

To create a signature in Thunderbird, go to "***Account settings***" and select the account for which you want to create a signature. You can enter your signature in the "***Signature text***" area. You can use both plain text and HTML for your signature. If you want to use HTML, activate the "***Use HTML***" checkbox.

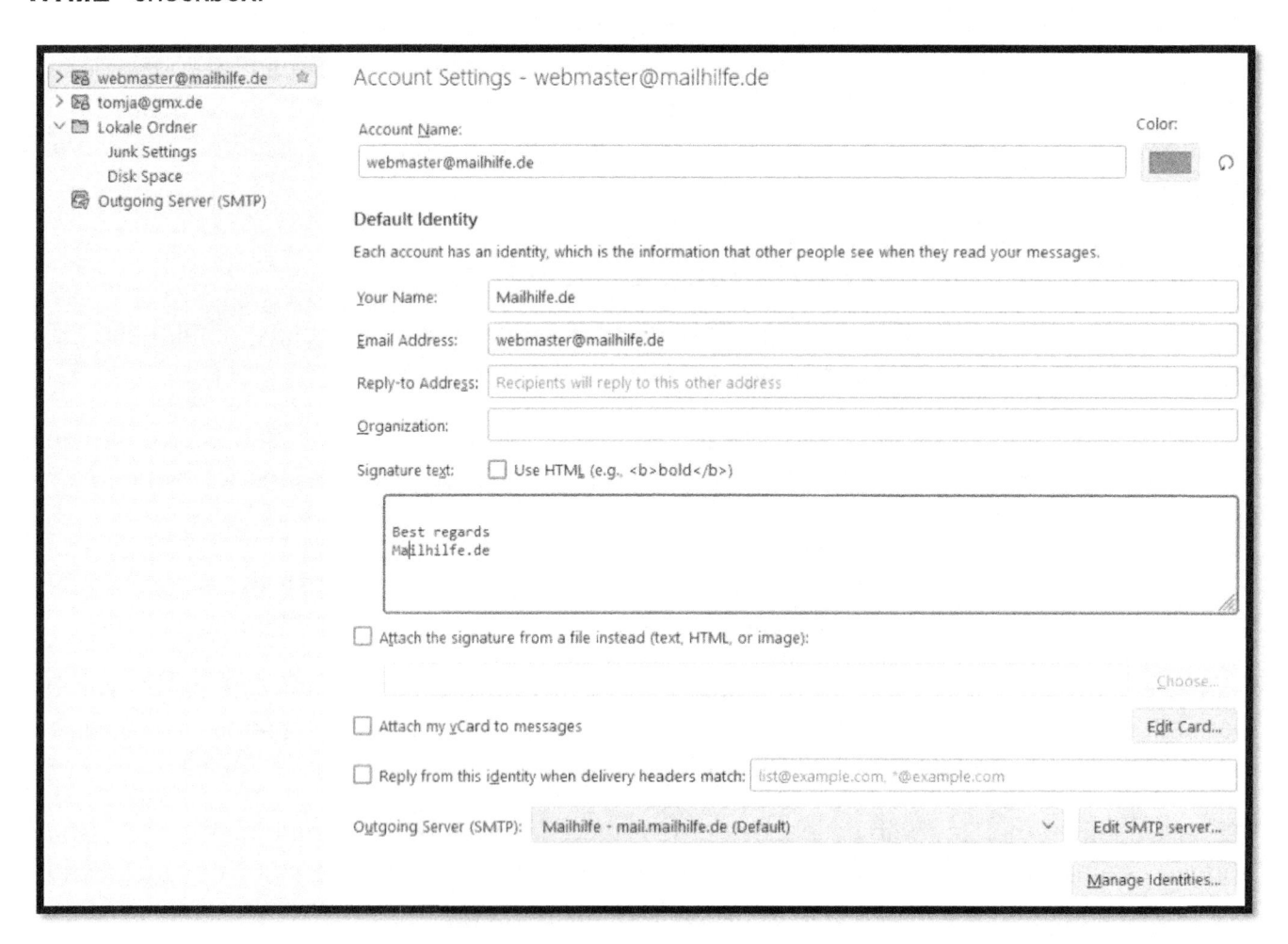

7.3.2 MULTIPLE SIGNATURES USE

If you have several e-mail accounts or want to use different signatures for different purposes, you can create and manage multiple signatures. You can define a separate signature for each account or create a signature and then add it manually to your emails.

7.3.3 ADDING A SIGNATURE TO EMAILS

By default, Thunderbird automatically adds the signature to the end of every email that you send with the corresponding account. However, you can change this setting by checking or unchecking the "***Hide signature on forwards and replies***" checkbox. If you want to add a signature to an email manually, you can do this by selecting the signature from the "***Insert***" menu.

7.4 RSS FEEDS AND NEWSGROUPS

In this section, you will learn how you can use RSS feeds and newsgroups in Thunderbird to optimize your news consumption and stay up-to-date.

7.3.4 DESIGNING A PROFESSIONAL SIGNATURE

A good email signature should be short and informative. It should include your name, position, contact details, and, if applicable, the name and website of your company. You can also include links to your social media profiles or other relevant resources. Make sure your signature is not too long or cluttered.

7.3.5 LEGAL ASPECTS

In some countries and industries, there are legal requirements for email signatures. These may, for example, require certain company in- formation or legal notices to be included. Make sure that your email signature meets all relevant legal requirements.

7.3.6 BUSINESS CARDS-SIGNATURES

In addition to the simple text or HTML signature, you can also create a business card signature in Thunderbird. To create a business card signature, go to the ***account settings and select*** the account for which you want to create a signature. Check the box "***Attach my vCard to messages***" and click on "***Edit card***" to select your signature.

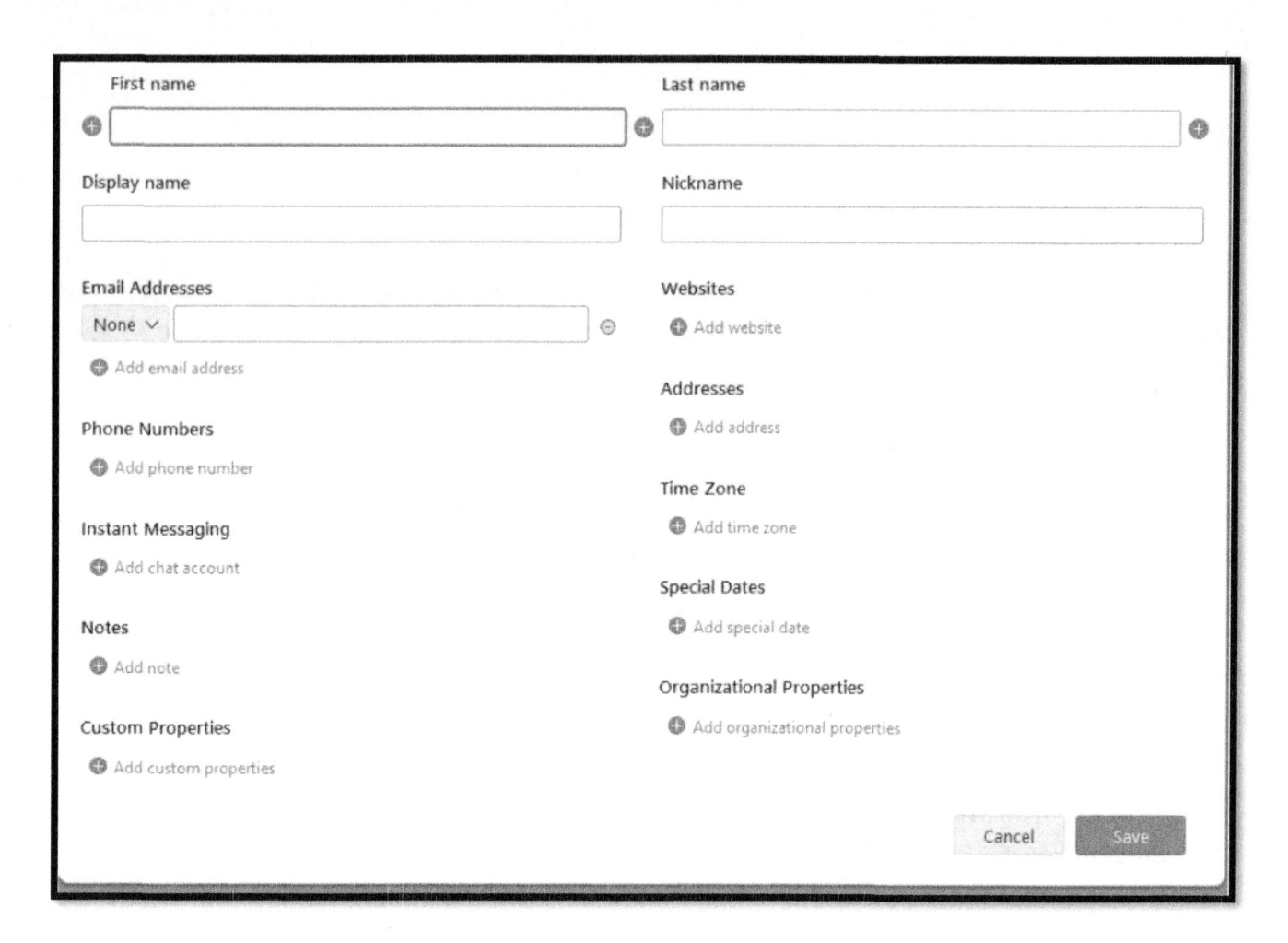

Edit the individual fields and then click on "*Save*.".

7.3.7 USING ADD-ONS TO

MANAGE SIGNATURES

There are various add-ons for Thunderbird that offer additional options and functions for managing signatures. management. Examples are *Signature Switch and Wise Stamp.* These add-ons can help you manage multiple signatures, improve the formatting of your signatures, or even add dynamic content such as quotes or RSS feeds to your signatures. into your signatures.

Thunderbird therefore offers a wide range of options for creating and managing e-mail signatures. to create and manage email signatures. Regardless of whether you prefer a simple text signature or a complex HTML signature with images and links, Thunderbird offers you the tools you need to create a professional and effective email signature.

7.4.1 RSS FEEDS

RSS feeds (Really Simple Syndication) are a handy tool to automatically receive the latest articles and updates from your favorite websites and blogs without having to visit them manually. Thunderbird allows you to subscribe to and manage RSS feeds directly in your email client. Find out how to subscribe to RSS feeds in Thunderbird here:

1. Open Thunderbird and right-click on your account name or an empty area under your accounts in the left pane. Select "***New***"> *"**Feed account**"*.

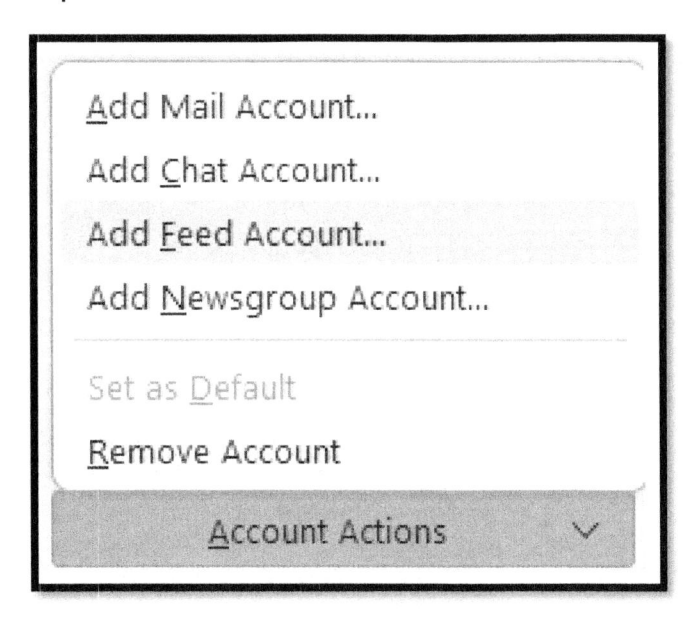

2. Enter a name for the feed account and click on "***Next***" and then on "***Finish***".

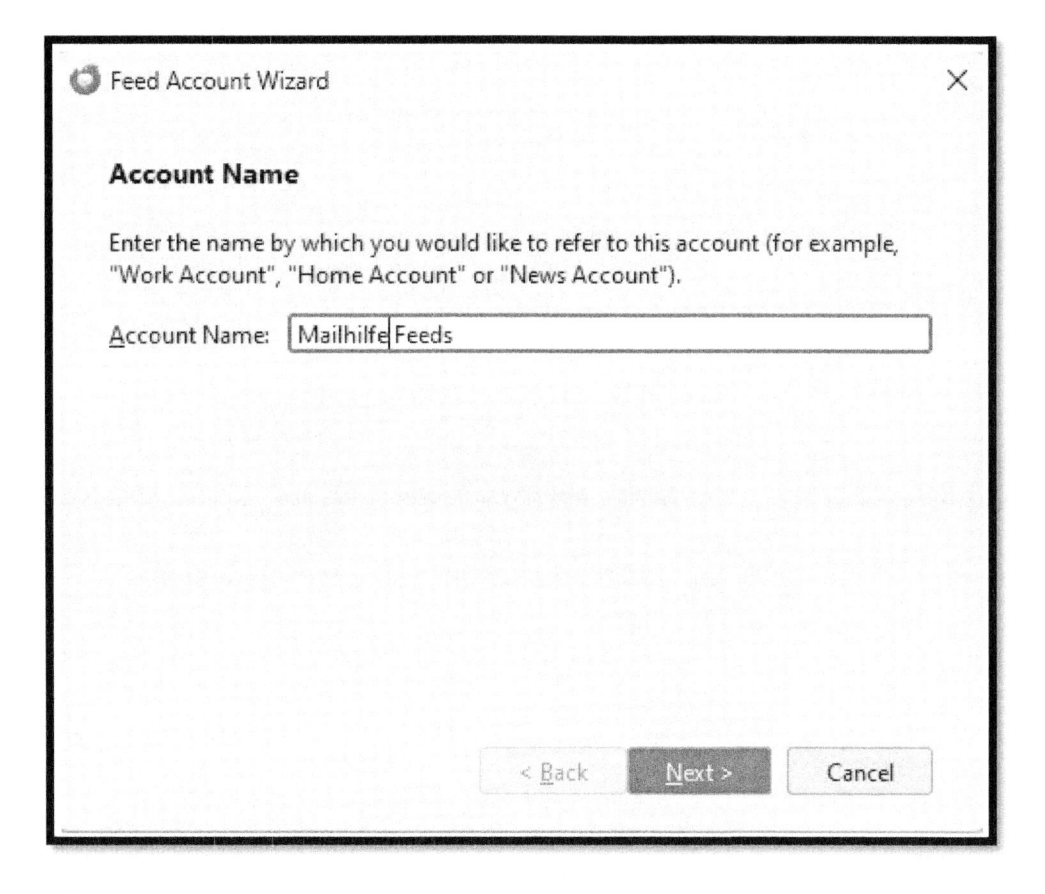

Feed Account Wizard

Summary

A summary of the information you entered is displayed below. Please check it before the account is created.

Account Name: Mailhilfe Feeds

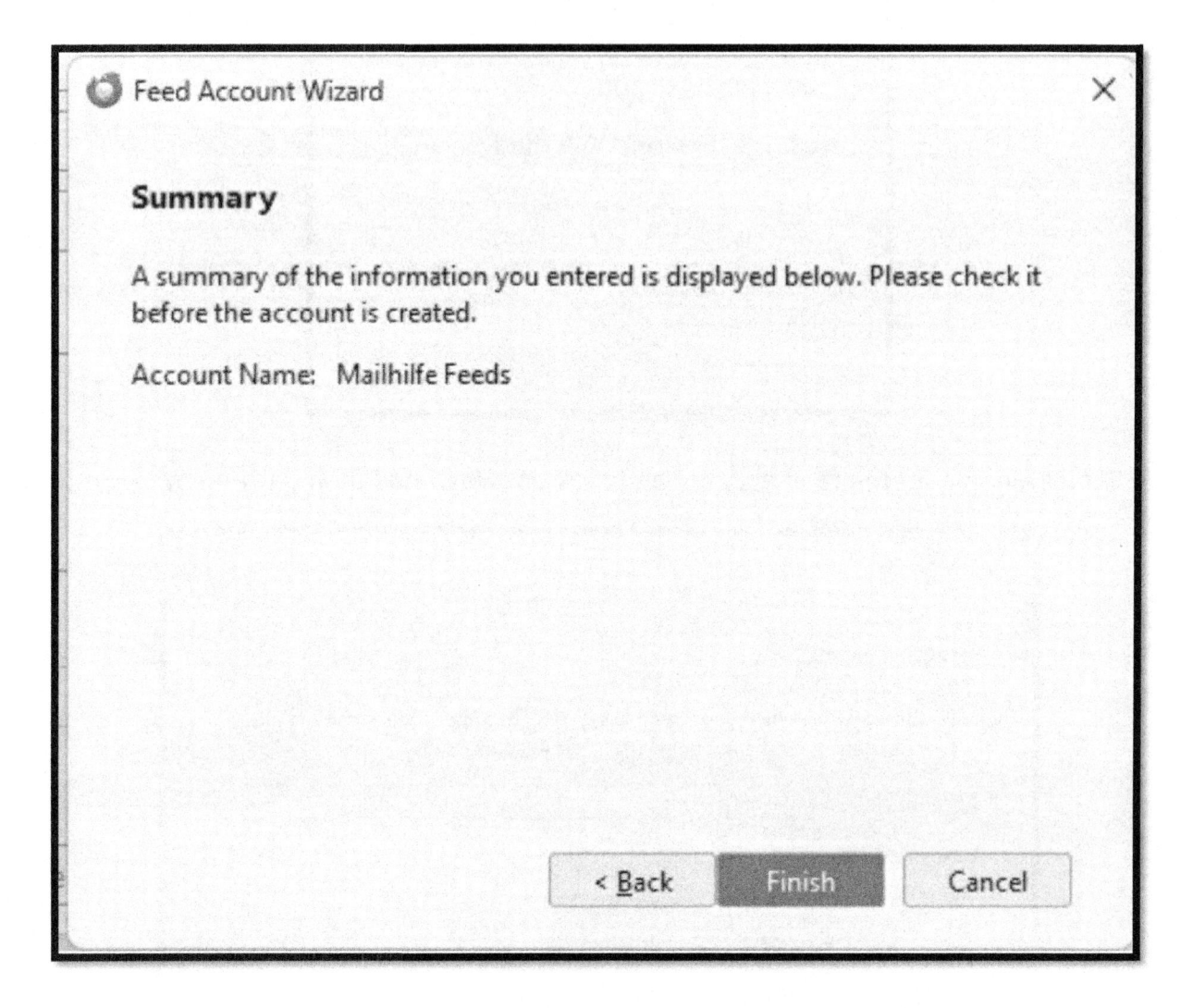

[< Back]   [Finish]   [Cancel]

3. Right—click on the newly created feed account and select "Subscribe".

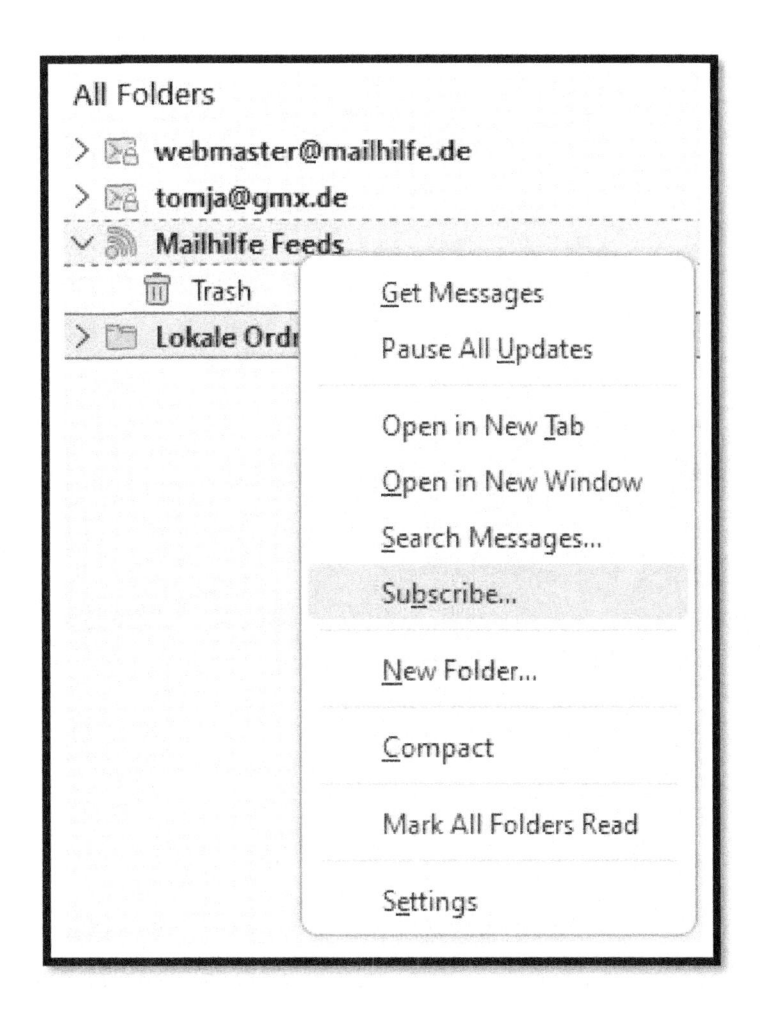

4. Enter the URL (https://www.mailhilfe.de/feed) of the desired RSS feed and click on and click on "**Add**" and then on "**Close**".

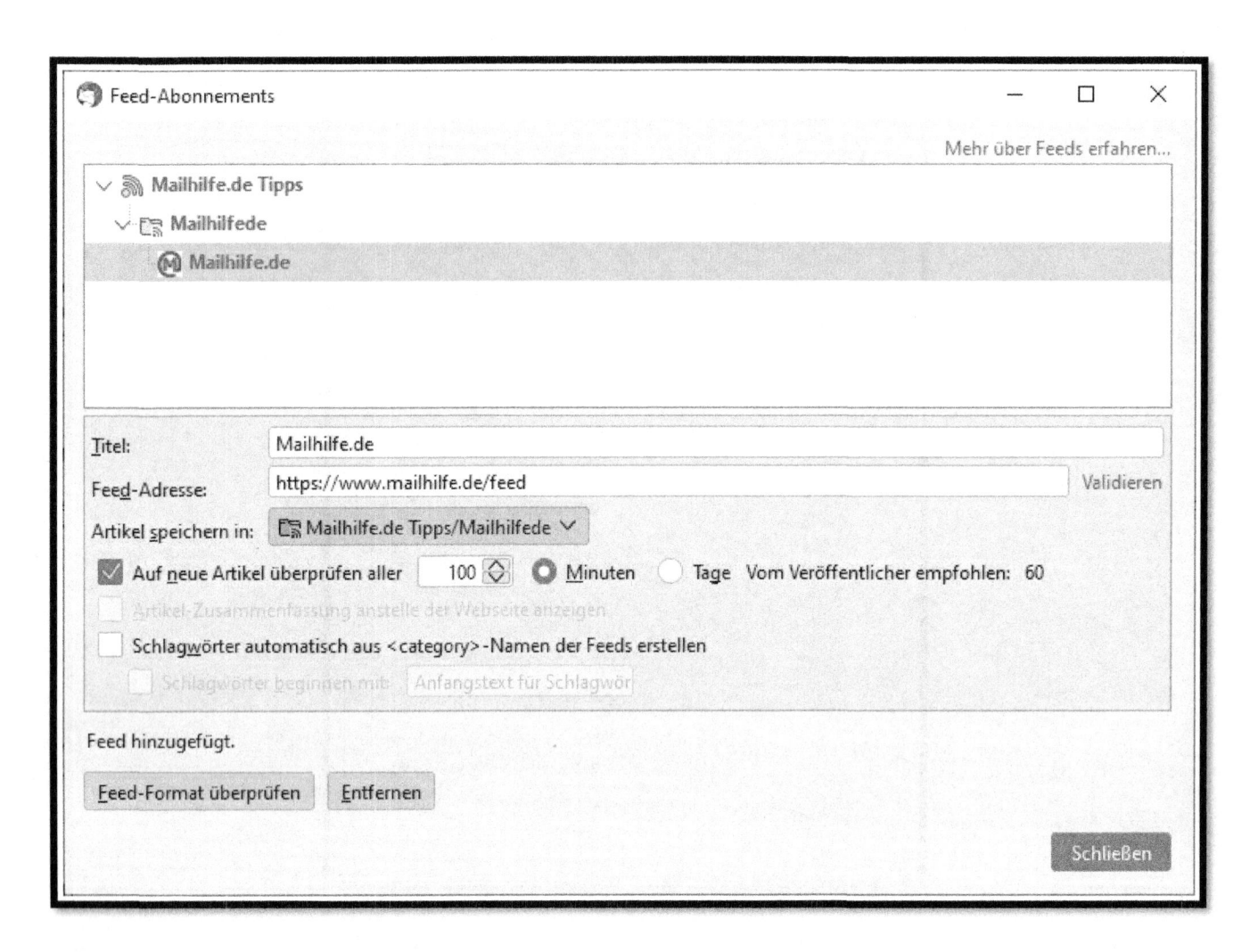

5. The latest articles of the RSS feed are now displayed in the feed account folder and updated automatically.

7.4.1 NEWSGROUP

1. Open Thunderbird and right-click on your account name or an empty area below your accounts in the left pane. Select "**New">" News group account".

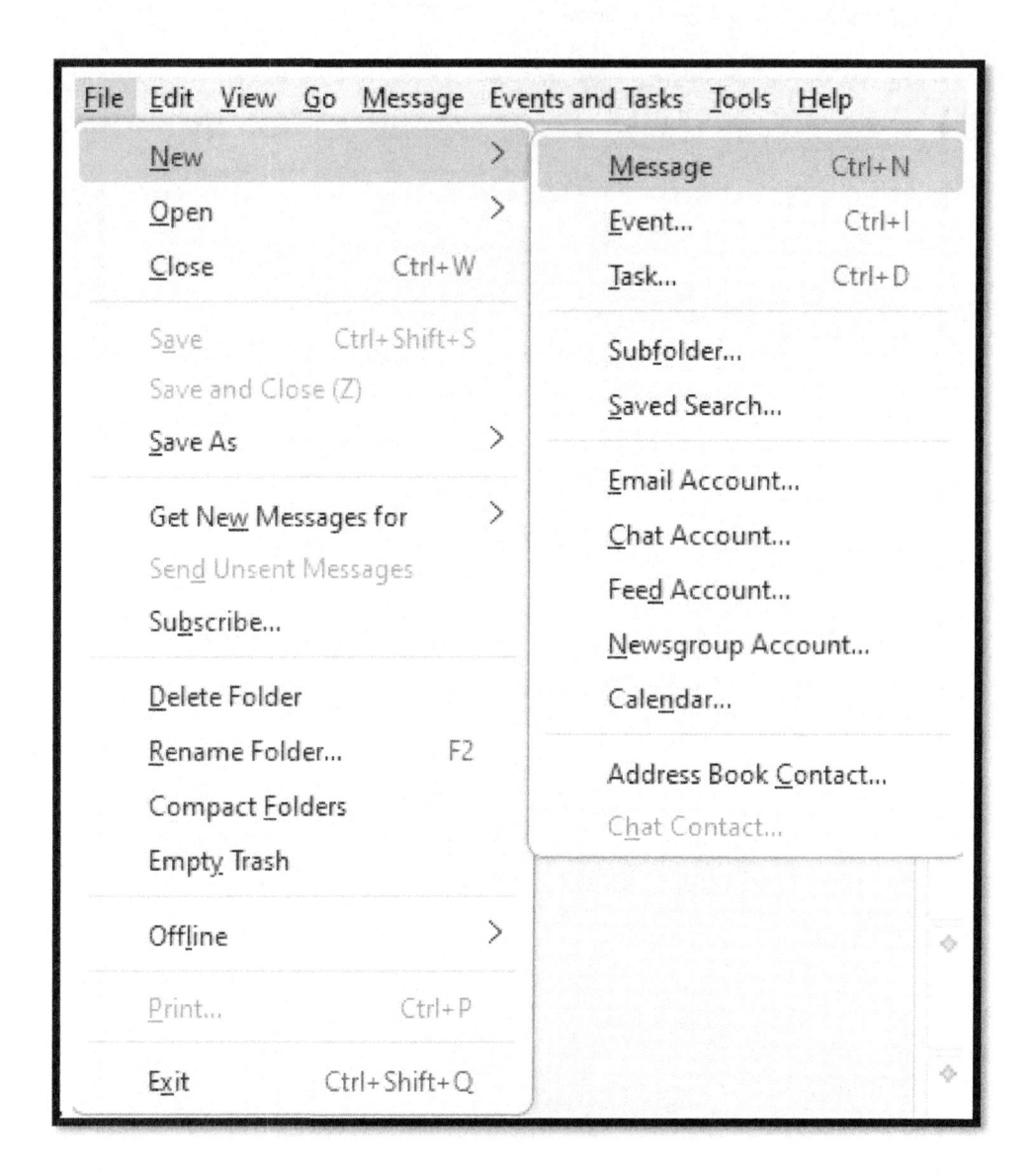

2. Enter a name and e-mail address for the feed account and click on **"Next"**.
3. Enter the URL of the desired newsgroup server and click on **"Next"**.
4. The subscribed groups are now displayed under the newsgroup account, and you can read and participate in discussions.

With RSS feeds and newsgroups in Thunderbird, you can manage your favorite content and discussions centrally and always stay up to date.

7.5 ADVANCED SEARCH AND FILTERS

This chapter introduces Thunderbird's advanced search and filter functions, which help you to manage your emails efficiently and find the information you need quickly.

7.5.1 ADVANCED SEARCH

The advanced search in Thunderbird allows you to find emails based on various criteria. You can search both within a single folder and across all folders and accounts. Here you can find out how to use the advanced search in Thunderbird:

1. Open Thunderbird and click on the magnifying glass icon in the toolbar, or press the key combination "**Ctrl + Shift + F"** (or "**Cmd + Shift + F**" on a Mac).

The "**Search messages**" window opens. Select the desired search area, e.g "**Search in all accounts and folders"** or "**Search in this folder only".**

Enter the search term in the empty white field.

2. You can add additional search criteria by clicking on the"+" button and selecting the desired options from the drop-down menus. For example, you can search by sender, recipient, subject, or date.
3. Click on "**Search" to start** the search. The search results are displayed in the lower part of the window. Double-click on an email to open it.

7.5.2 FILTERS AND RULES

With the filter- and rule-functions of Thunderbird, you can automatically organize and manage your emails by performing certain actions based on selected criteria. For example, you can automatically move emails from certain senders to a specific folder or delete unwanted emails directly. Here you can find out how to create filters and rules in Thunderbird:

1. Open Thunderbird and click on the menu icon (three horizontal bars) in the top right-hand corner. Select "**Tools"> "Message Filter.**".

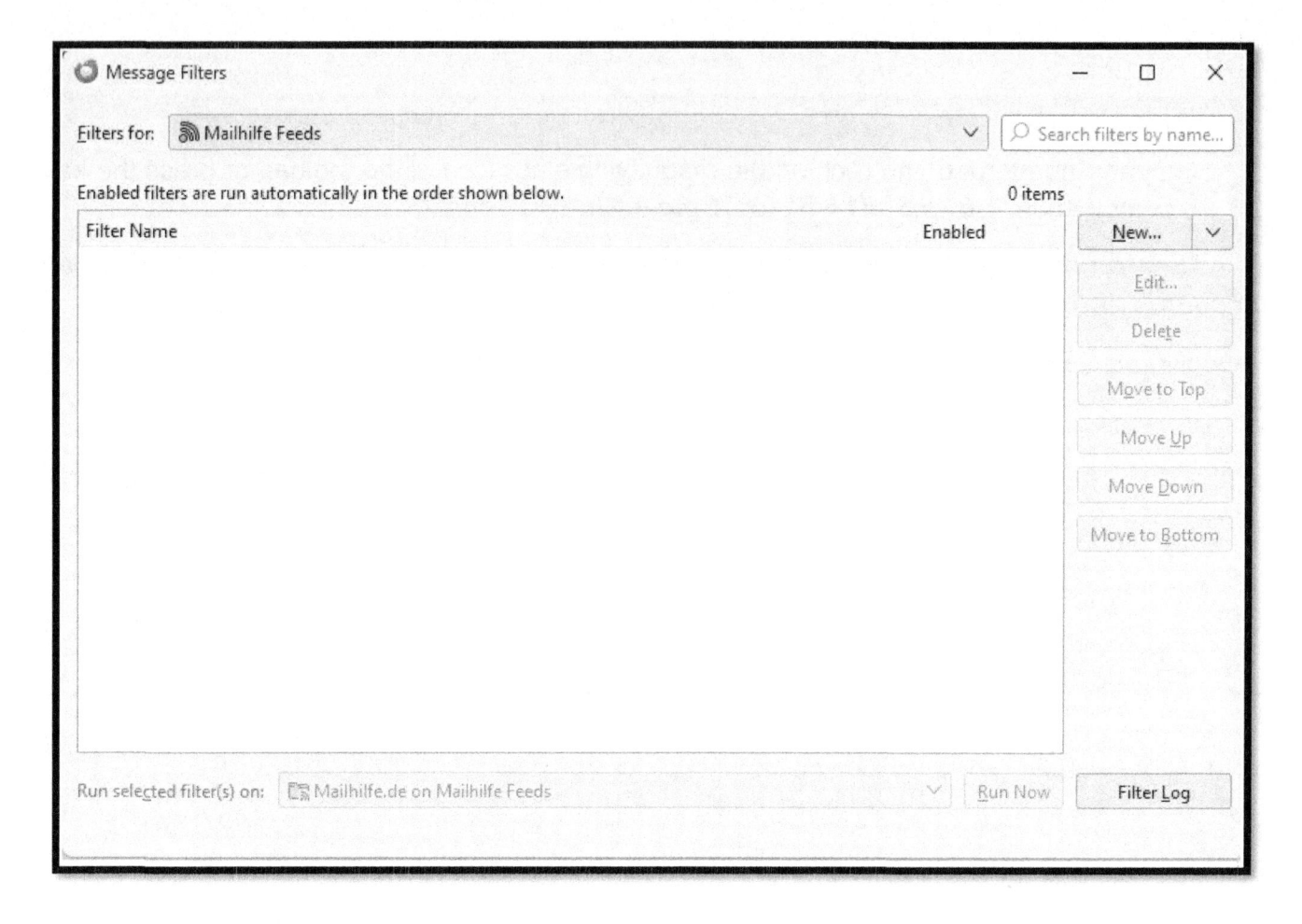

2. In the "Manage filters Manage filters" window, click on "**New**" to create a new filter.
3. Enter a name for the filter and select the desired conditions from the drop-down menus. You can add multiple conditions by clicking on the "**+**" button.
4. Select the desired actions to be applied to emails that meet the defined conditions. You can add multiple actions by clicking on the "**+**" button.
5. Click on "**OK**" to save the filter. to save the filter. The filter is now automatically applied to new emails that meet the specified conditions.

An example of a filter would be to move all emails from a specific sender to a specific folder. To do this, set the "***From***" condition to the sender's email address and select "***Move to folder***" as the action, followed by the selection of the desired target folder.

7.5.3 FILTER EXCEPTIONS AND PRIORITIES

In certain cases, it may be necessary to exclude certain emails from the application of the filter rules. You can create exceptions by defining additional conditions with the option "All conditions" or "At least one condition.".

For example, you could create a filter that moves all emails from a specific sender to a folder, unless they contain a specific keyword in the subject. In this case, set the "***From***" condition to the sender's email address and the "***Subject does not contain***" condition to the desired key word. Then activate "***At least one condition***" to ensure that both conditions must be met before the action is executed.

You can also set the priority of your filters by moving them up or down in the "Manage filters" window. Filters higher up in the list are applied first. This is helpful if you have several filters that could influence each other.

7.5.4 FILTER APPLY MANUALLY

In the default setting, Thunderbird applies filters automatically to new emails. In some cases, you may want to apply filters manually to existing emails. To do this, open the "**Manage filters**" window, select the desired filter, and click "Run now." You can also select multiple filters and click "**Run all selected**" to run all selected filters at the same time.

To summarize, Thunderbird's advanced search and filter features provide a powerful way to efficiently manage your emails and find exactly the information you need. By customizing and using these features, you can optimize your email workflow and save time.

7.5.5 QUICK SEARCH

Another useful feature of Thunderbird is the quick search, which allows you to search your emails quickly and easily without opening the "Advanced search" window. The quick search is located directly above the list of your emails and is indicated by the magnifying glass icon.

If you want to use the quick search, simply enter your search term in the field and press Enter. Thunderbird will then search the current folder for matches and display the results in the email list. You can also use the quick search to search for emails according to specific criteria, such as sender, recipient, or subject. To do this, enter the corresponding prefix (e.g. "from" or "subject:") before your search term.

7.5.6 SEARCH OPERATORS

To further refine your search, you can use search operators in the quick search and advanced search. These operators allow you to form late, more precise search queries and filter the results better. Some common search operators are

- **AND**: Displays results that contain all specified search terms (e.g., "invoice AND rent").
- **OR**: Displays results that contain at least one of the specified search terms (e.g. "invoice OR rent").
- **NOT**: Displays results that do not contain one of the specified search terms (e.g., "invoice NOT rent").
- **""**(quotation marks): Displays results that contain the exact phrase within the quotation marks (e.g. "invoice rent").
- **()** (square brackets): Combines search operators and terms to formulate complex search queries (e.g."(bill AND rent) OR (bill AND electricity)").

With these search operators, you can create complex search queries and search your emails even more efficiently.

7.5.7 SAVED SEARCH FOLDERS

Another useful feature of Thunderbird is the saved search folders. These allow you to save user-defined search queries so that you can quickly execute them again at any time. To create a search folder, proceed as follows:

- Right-click on your account name or an empty area below your accounts and select "*Search messages.*".

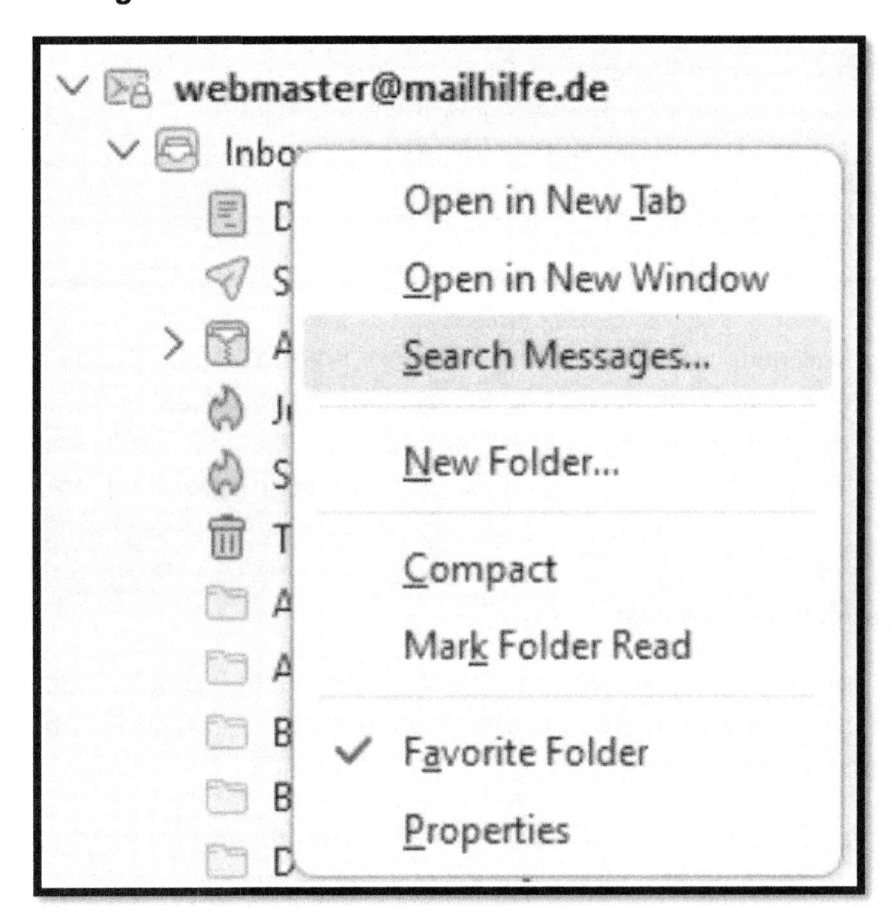

- Enter a search term and select the conditions.

- Then click "**Save as virtual folder...**"
- Enter a name for the search folder and select the desired search criteria. Click on "**Create**" to save the search folder.

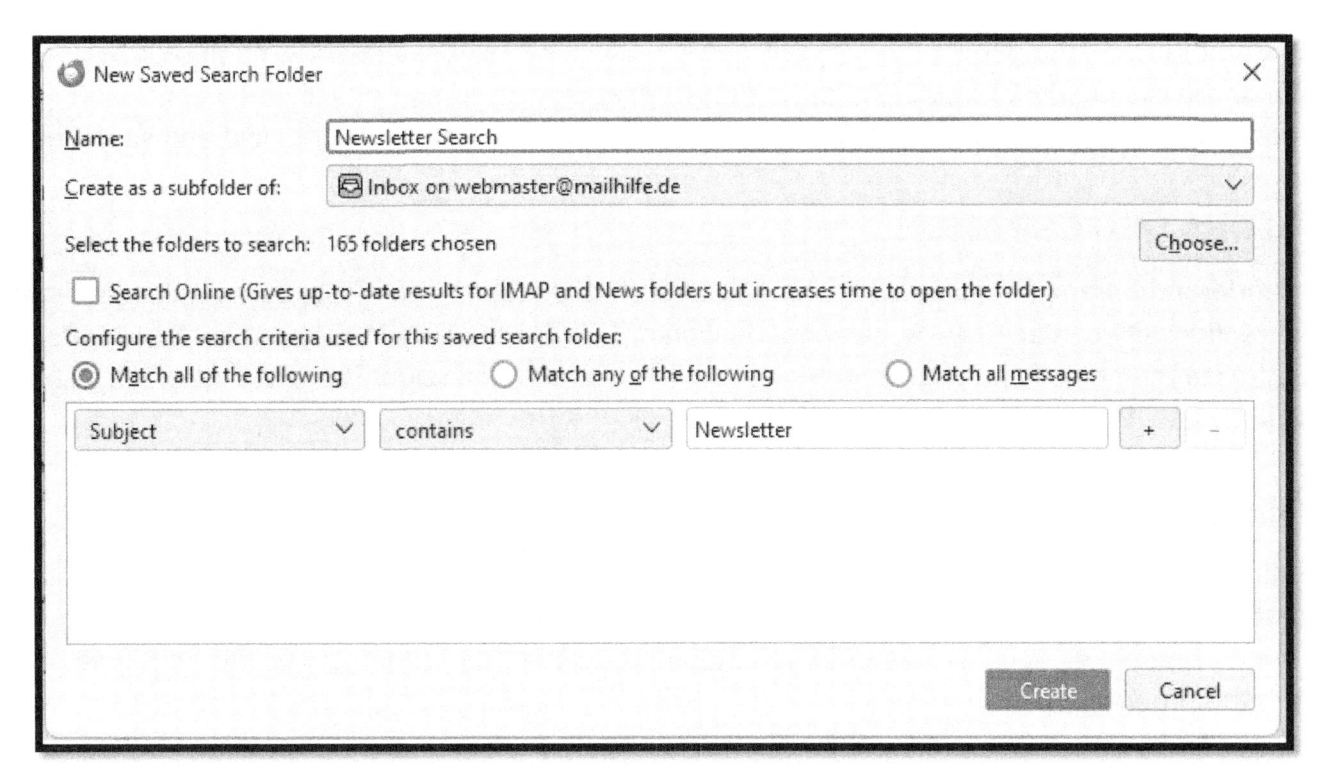

The saved search folder now appears in your folder list. You can run the saved search again at any time by clicking on it.

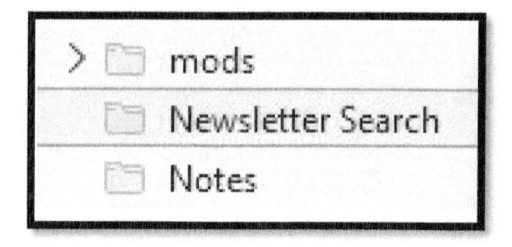

Overall, Thunderbird's advanced search and filter functions offer you numerous ways to manage your emails effectively and find exactly the information you need. By customizing and using these features, you can optimize your email workflow and save time.

7.5.8 SEARCH SENT E-MAILS

Sometimes you may want to search through your sent emails to track past communications or find information that you have sent to others. In Thunderbird, you can search your sent emails in the same way as your received emails. Simply select the "***Sent***" folder or another folder containing your sent emails as the search area and perform the search as usual.

7.5.9 SEARCH IN NEWSGROUPS AND RSS FEEDS

Thunderbird also supports searching in newsgroups and RSS feeds so that you can quickly find important information in these channels. To search in newsgroups or RSS feeds, select the desired folder or feed as the search area and use the advanced search or quick search as usual.

To summarize, Thunderbird's advanced search and filter features provide numerous ways to effectively manage your email and other message sources and find exactly the information you need. By customizing and using these features, you can optimize your workflow and save time.

7.6 CHAT-INTEGRATION

Thunderbird offers an integrated chat feature that enables seamless communication and interaction with contacts on various chat networks. This feature was introduced to allow users to centralize their email and chat communication in one place and supports various protocols such as IRC, XMPP, Google Talk, and Twitter.

7.6.1 SETTING UP CHAT ACCOUNTS

Setting up a chat account in Thunderbird is straightforward. Under "***File*** -> *"New"* -> *"Create chat account,"*** you can select the desired network, enter your account details, and log in. Thunderbird saves your access data securely and logs you in automatically the next time you start the program.

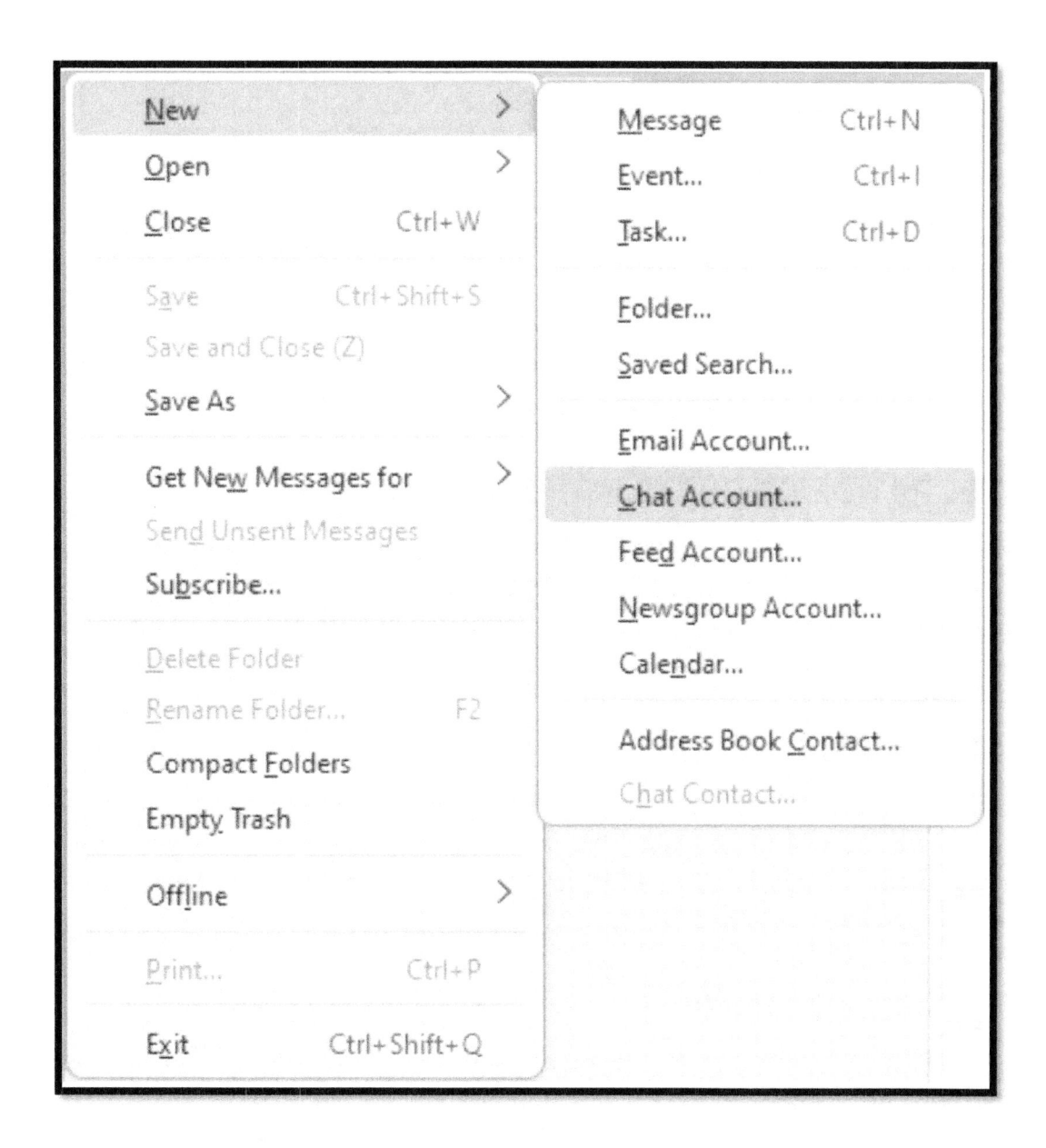

7.6.2 USING THE CHAT

The chat is integrated into the Thunderbird window so that you can easily switch between email and chat. You can open individual chats in tabs and navigate between them, similar to what you are used to with web browsers. You can also activate notifications for new chat messages to stay up to date.

7.6.3 CONTACTS AND MANAGE GROUPS

You can manage your chat contacts directly in Thunderbird. You can add, delete, edit, and even create groups to better organize your contacts. You can also see the online status of your contacts and set your own status.

7.6.4 SEARCH CHAT LOGS

Thunderbird saves your chat logs and allows you to search through them. This is particularly useful if you are looking for specific information or a specific chat history. You can access the search via the menu "*Edit*" -> "*Search*"-> "*Search in chats.*".

7.6.5 INTEGRATION OF CHATS INTHE GLOBAL SEARCH

Your chats are also integrated into Thunderbird's global search. This means that you can use the search field at the top right of Thunderbird to search not only your emails but also your chats. This is particularly useful if you are looking for information but are not sure whether you received it by email or chat.

7.6.6 CHAT PROTOCOLS

The chat logs in Thunderbird are an excellent feature that allows you to save the history of your conversations and access them later. This feature is especially useful if you have important information in a conversation and need to review it at a later time. You can access your chat logs by selecting "*View*" -> "*Chat logs*".

7.6.7 CHAT NOTIFICATIONS

Thunderbird offers notifications to inform you about new chat messages. You can customize the settings for these notifications to ensure that you are only notified when you want to be. Enable or disable the notifications, change the sound, and even set whether the notifications are displayed when Thunderbird is minimized.

7.6.8 EMOJIS AND RICH TEXT FORMATTING

Thunderbird Chat also supports the use of emojis and rich text formatting, so you can customize your messages to your liking. To insert emojis into your messages, click on the emoji icon in the message input bar, and to change the formatting, use the appropriate keyboard shortcuts.

Overall, the chat integration in Thunderbird provides a convenient and efficient way to centralize and manage your chat communications. With the ability to support multiple chat accounts, powerful search functions, and a simple user interface, Thunderbird enables seamless integration of email and chat communication.

CHAPTER 8: ENSURING EMAIL SECURITY AND ENCRYPTION

Email encryption is an important aspect of digital security as it helps to maintain the confidentiality and integrity of messages and prevent unauthorized access to sensitive information. This chapter covers the basics of email encryption in Thunderbird and the various techniques that can be used to secure your emails.

8.1 BASICS OF E-MAIL ENCRYPTION

Email encryption is the conversion of plain text messages into an encrypted code that can only be decrypted and read by authorized persons. This is achieved by using cryptographic algorithms and keys to alter messages so that they become unreadable unless the recipient has the correct key to decrypt them. There are two main types of email encryption: symmetric encryption and asymmetric encryption (also known as public key encryption).

8.1.1 SYMMETRIC ENCRYPTION

In symmetric encryption, a single key is used to encrypt and decrypt messages. The sender and recipient of the message must use the same key, i.e., they must find a secure way to exchange the key without it being intercepted by third parties. Symmetric encryption is usually faster than asymmetric encryption but carries the risk of the key being compromised during the exchange.

8.1.2 ASYMMETRIC ENCRYPTION

In asymmetric encryption, also known as public-key encryption, two different keys are used: a public and a private key. The public key is used to encrypt messages while the private key is used to decrypt them. Each user has a pair of keys, and the public key can be freely shared without compromising the security of the communication. Asymmetric encryption offers a higher level of security than symmetric encryption, but is generally slower and more computationally intensive.

8.2 E-MAIL ENCRYPTION WITH THUNDERBIRD

Thunderbird offers various methods for e-mail encryption, including the integration of Pretty Good Privacy (PGP) and the use of Secure/Multipurpose Internet Mail Extensions (S/MIME).

8.2.1 PRETTY GOOD PRIVACY (PGP)

PGP is a popular email encryption protocol that uses asymmetric encryption to protect the confidentiality of messages. Thunderbird supports PGP encryption via the Enigmail-extension used in earlier versions of Thunderbird or via the built-in OpenPGP functionality in newer versions. To use OpenPGP in Thunderbird, you must first create or import a key pair and then share your public key with your contacts so that they can send you encrypted messages.

1. Create or import key pair Go to "***Thunderbird > Tools > OpenPGP Key Manager***" and select either "***Generate***" or under "***File*** > *"**Import key**"* to add existing keys.

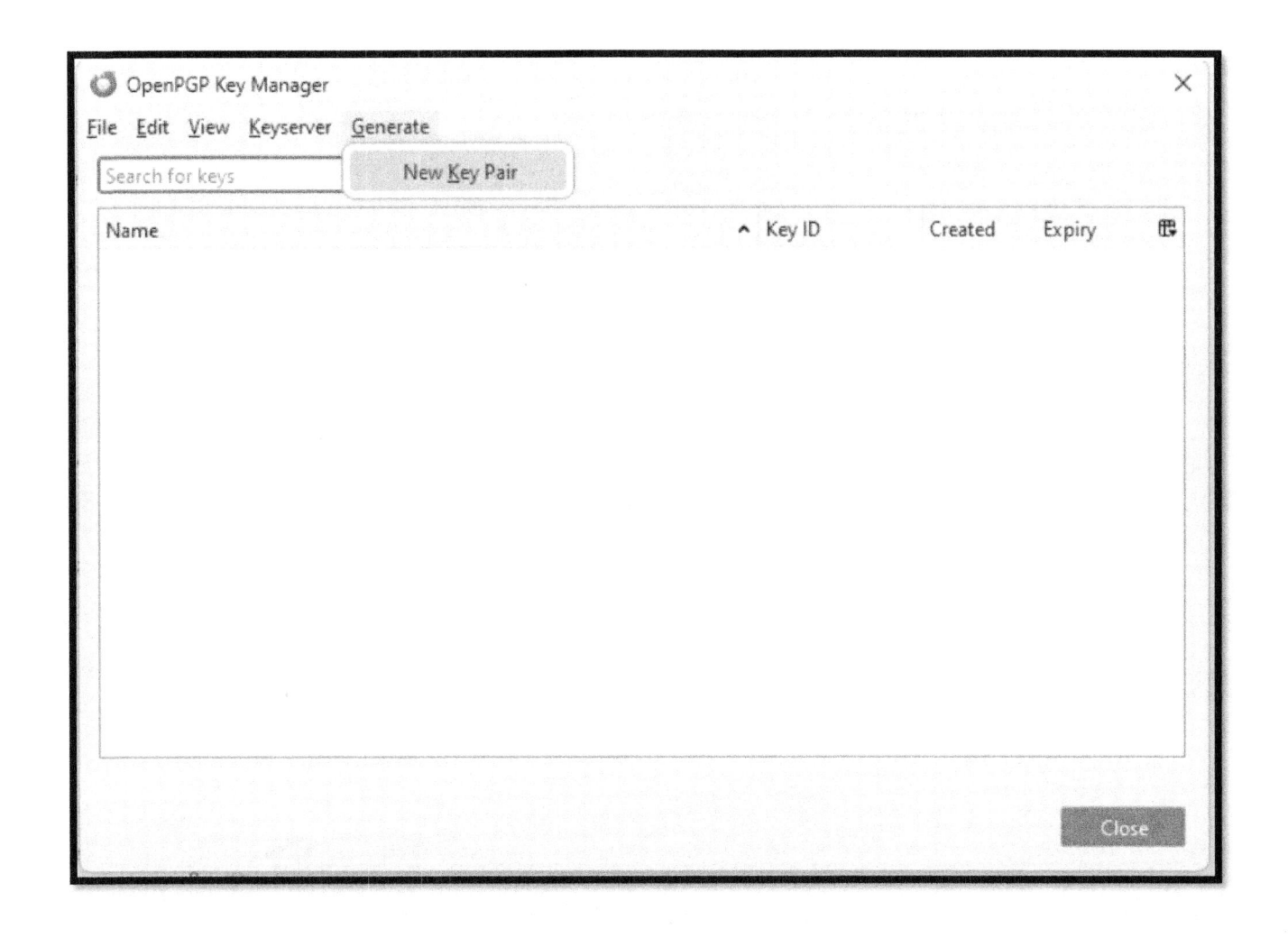

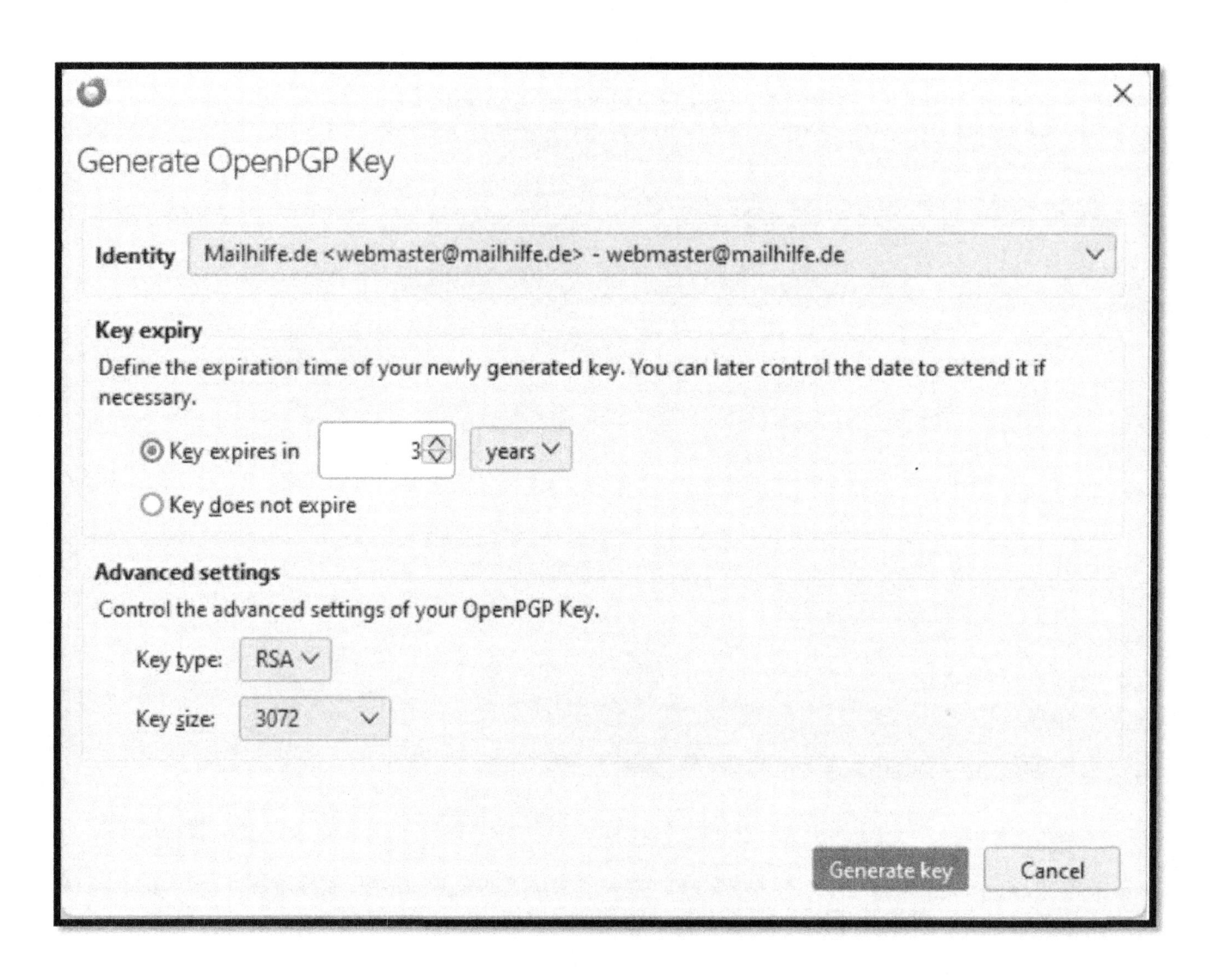

Generate OpenPGP Key

Identity | Mailhilfe.de <webmaster@mailhilfe.de> - webmaster@mailhilfe.de

Key expiry

Define the expiration time of your newly generated key. You can later control the date to extend it if necessary.

- ◉ K__e__y expires in [3] [years ∨]
- ○ Key __d__oes not expire

Advanced settings

Control the advanced settings of your OpenPGP Key.

Key __t__ype: [RSA ∨]

Key __s__ize: [3072 ∨]

[Generate key] [Cancel]

> **Key generation may take up to several minutes to com**... Add a Personal OpenPGP Key for webmaster@r
> key generation is in progress. Actively browsing or performing disk-intensive operations during key
> generation will replenish the 'randomness pool' and speed-up the process. You will be alerted when
> key generation is completed.

Generate public and secret key for Mailhilfe.de **"webmaster@mailhilfe.de"**?

Cancel   Confirm

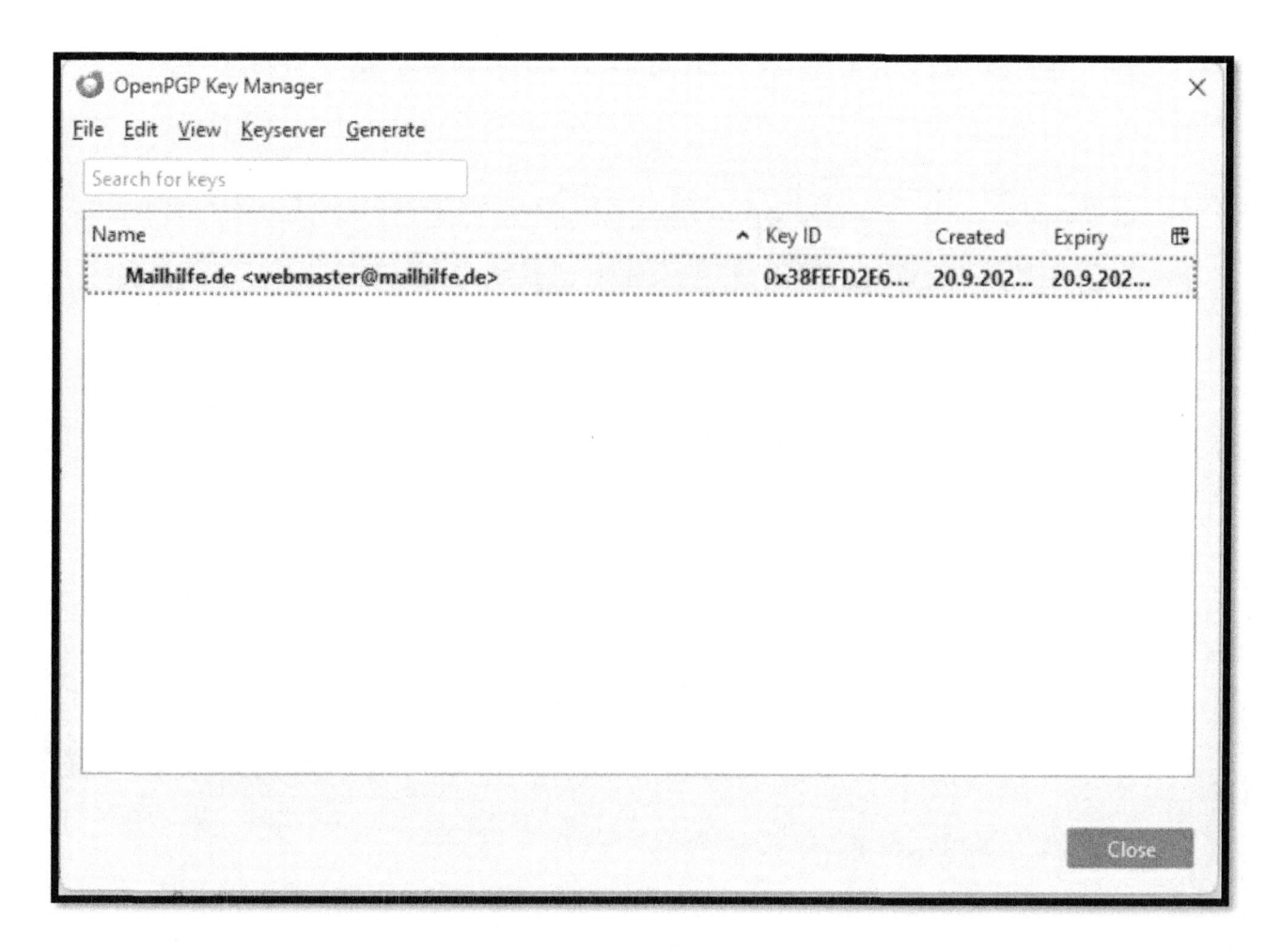

2. Manage keys: You can display, export, import, and manage your keys in the OpenPGP key management. Share your public key with your contacts by sending it by e-mail or publishing it on a key server.

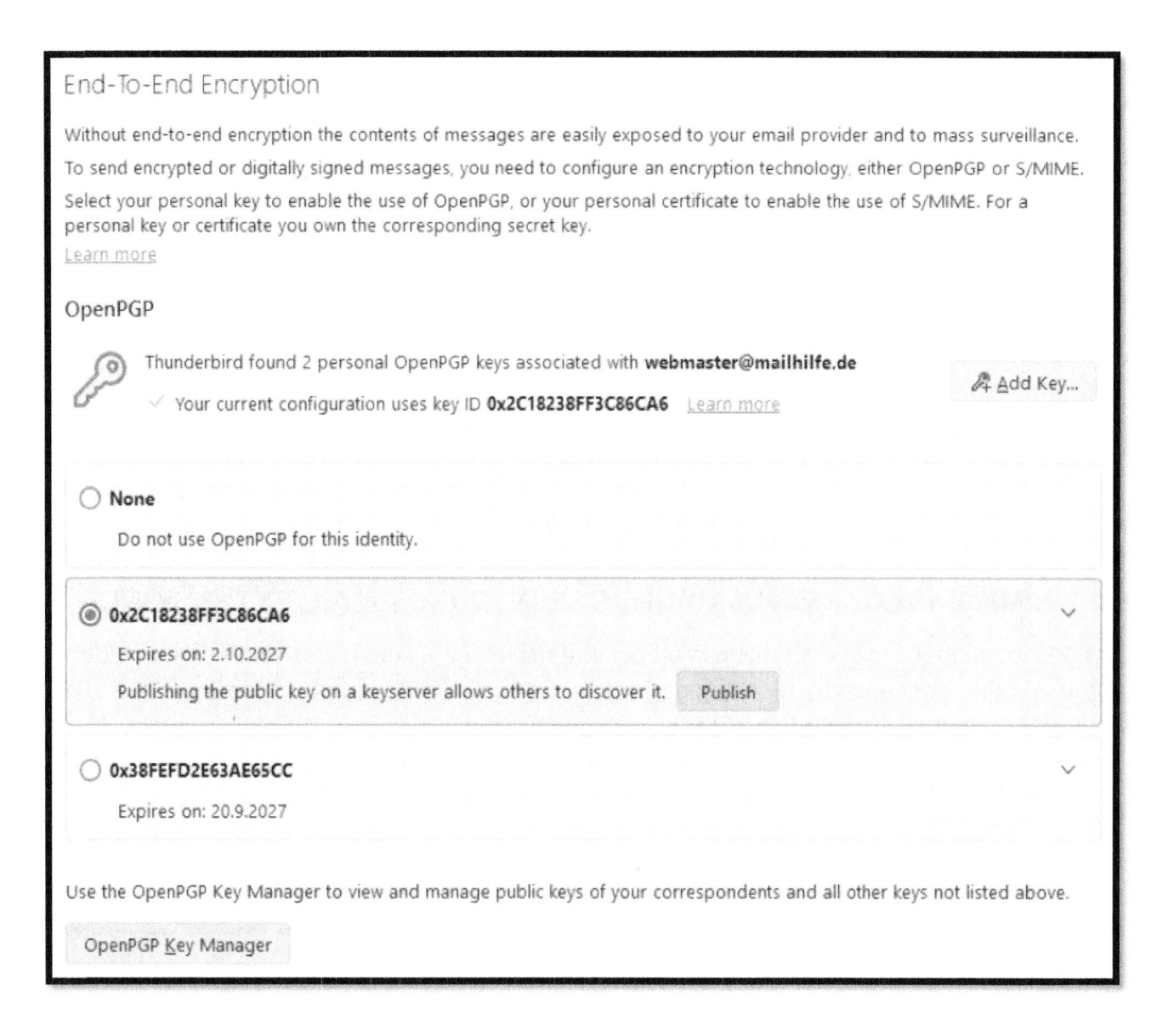

End-To-End Encryption

Without end-to-end encryption the contents of messages are easily exposed to your email provider and to mass surveillance. To send encrypted or digitally signed messages, you need to configure an encryption technology, either OpenPGP or S/MIME. Select your personal key to enable the use of OpenPGP, or your personal certificate to enable the use of S/MIME. For a personal key or certificate you own the corresponding secret key.
Learn more

OpenPGP

Thunderbird found 2 personal OpenPGP keys associated with **webmaster@mailhilfe.de**
✓ Your current configuration uses key ID **0x2C18238FF3C86CA6**   Learn more

🔑 Add Key...

○ **None**
   Do not use OpenPGP for this identity.

◉ **0x2C18238FF3C86CA6**
   Expires on: 2.10.2027
   Publishing the public key on a keyserver allows others to discover it.   [Publish]

○ **0x38FEFD2E63AE65CC**
   Expires on: 20.9.2027

Use the OpenPGP Key Manager to view and manage public keys of your correspondents and all other keys not listed above.

[OpenPGP Key Manager]

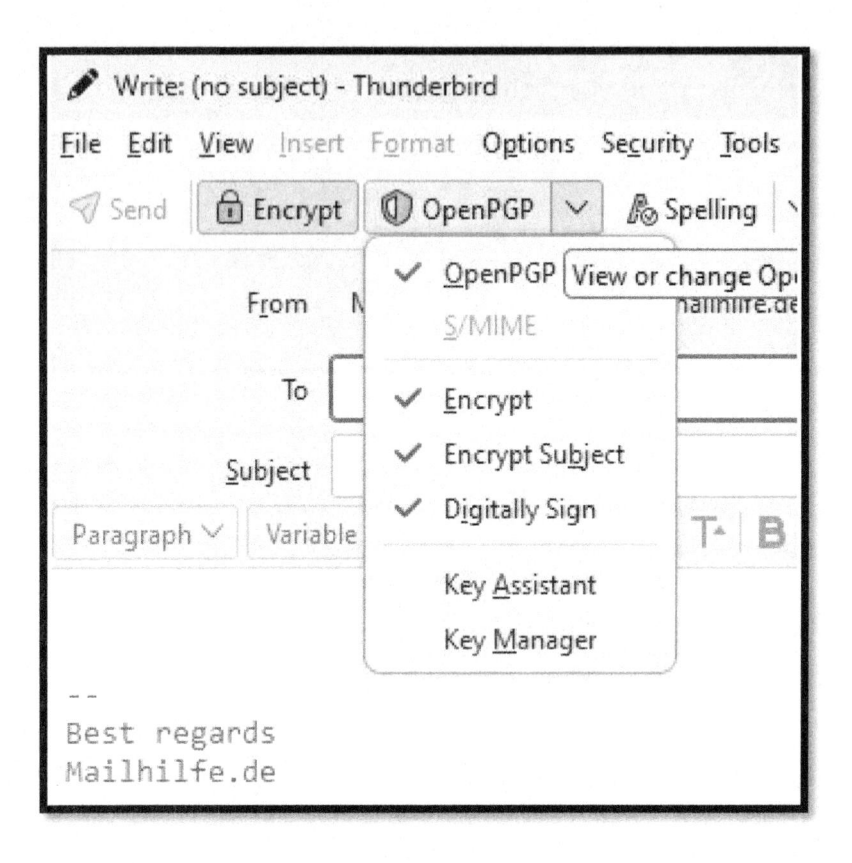

3. To encrypt the message with the recipient's public key. Make sure that you have the recipient's public key in your key management.

8.2.2 S/MIME (SECURE/MULTIPURPOSE INTERNET MAIL EXTENSIONS)

S/MIME is another email encryption protocol that uses digital certificates to confirm the identity of the sender and encrypt messages. To use S/MIME in Thunderbird, you need a digital certificate issued by a trusted certification authority (CA).

1. Apply for a certificate. Apply for a digital certificate from a CA that issues S/MIME-certificates, e.g. Sectigo, GlobalSign, or DigiCert.
2. Install the certificate: Import the certificate into Thunderbird under *"Tools> Settings> Privacy&: Security > Certificates."* and click on *"Manage certificates."*.

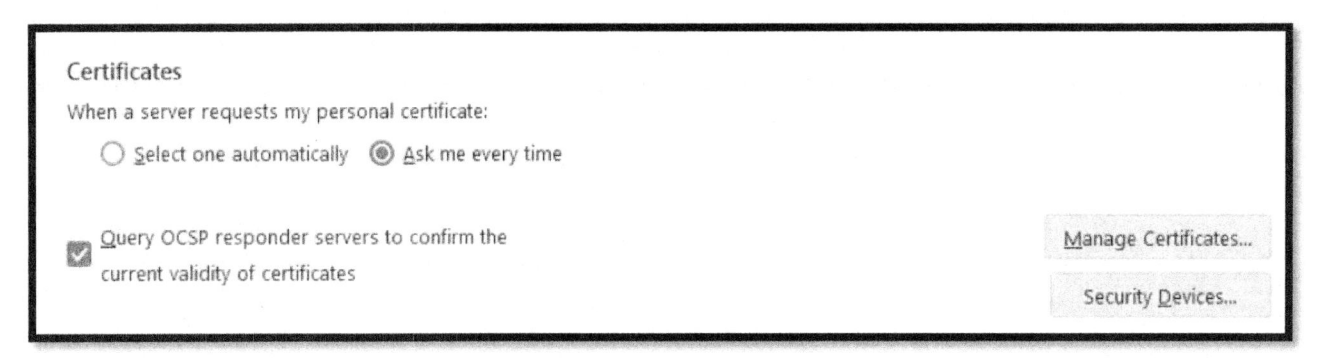

Select "*Import*" and navigate to the file that contains your certificate.

Certificate Manager				
Your Certificates	Authentication Decisions	People	Servers	**Authorities**

You have certificates on file that identify these certificate authorities

Certificate Name	Security Device
∨ ACCV	
ACCVRAIZ1	Builtin Object Token
∨ Actalis S.p.A./03358520967	
Actalis Authentication Root CA	Builtin Object Token

View...   Edit Trust...   **Import...**   Export...   Delete or Distrust...

OK

3. Sending encrypted emails: When composing an e-mail, you can activate the "***Sign***" and "***Encrypt***" options in the "***Security***" menu to sign and encrypt the message with your S/MIME-certificate to sign and encrypt the message. Make sure that you have the recipient's S/MIME certificate in your address book.

In short, email encryption is an essential tool to ensure the confidentiality and security of your electronic communications. Thunderbird offers various options for implementing email encryption, including PGP and S/MIME which allow users to protect confidential messages and ensure the integrity of their communications. By using encryption protocols such as PGP and S/MIME, you can ensure that your emails can only be read by authorized recipients and that your personal and business information is protected from unauthorized access.

8.3 RECOMMENDATIONS FOR ENCRYPTION

To further increase the security of your e-mail communication, you should observe the following best practices for e-mail encryption:

1. **Store keys and certificates securely:** Make sure that your private keys and digital certificates are stored securely and do not fall into the hands of unauthorized persons. Make regular backup copies of your keys and certificates and keep them in a safe place.
2. **Use trusted certification authorities:** Only use digital certificates from trusted certificate authorities (CAs) and make sure that your contacts do the same. do the same. This way, you can be sure that the certificates you use are genuine and secure.
3. **Update your encryption techniques:** Make sure your encryption tools and protocols are up-to-date to avoid security gaps and vulnerabilities. Update your Thunderbird software regularly and install all recommended security updates.

4. awareness-raising and training: Raise awareness among your colleagues, employees, and contacts of the importance of email encryption and provide training to ensure that everyone is using encryption technologies correctly and effectively.
5. **Use VPN** and secure connections: In addition to email encryption, use a Virtual Private Network (VPN) and secure connections such as HTTPS to protect your online activity and keep your data safe from potential eavesdropping.

By following these best practices, you can further improve the security of your email communications and protect your confidential information from unauthorized access and misuse. At a time when data protection and digital security are becoming increasingly important, email encryption is an indispensable tool for protecting your privacy and that of your contacts. protect your privacy and that of your contacts.

CHAPTER 9: TROUBLESHOOTING AND SUPPORT TIPS

Although Thunderbird is a reliable and user-friendly email program, problems can occasionally occur. If you have difficulties setting up your account, receive error messages, or simply cannot find a function, it is important to know how to solve these problems.

The ninth chapter of this book is about troubleshooting and support for Thunderbird. Here you will find detailed instructions for diagnosing and fixing common problems as well as advice in case you need further help.

We'll start with some basic troubleshooting strategies that can help you identify the cause of a problem and find possible solutions. This includes things like checking your internet connection, updating Thunderbird and its extensions, checking your settings, and reading error messages.

Next, we'll look at some specific problems that commonly occur when using Thunderbird and provide instructions on how to fix them. These include problems with receiving and sending emails, problems with the display of emails, problems with extensions, and much more.

Finally, we will discuss how to get help if you cannot solve a problem yourself. This includes dealing with Thunderbird support, using the Thunderbird community, and seeking professional help.

Regardless of your technical knowledge, after reading this chapter you should be better able to effectively solve problems with Thunderbird and get the most out of this powerful email program.

9.1 COMMON PROBLEMS AND SOLUTIONS

This section covers some of the most common problems that users may encounter and possible solutions.

9.1.1 E-MAILS CANNOT BE SENT OR RECEIVED.

This is a common problem that can have various causes. Here are some troubleshooting steps:

1. **Check your internet connection:** First, make sure that your device has a working internet connection. To do this, open a website in your browser. If there are any problems with the Internet connection, you must rectify these before continuing.
2. **Check your account settings:** If your internet connection is fine, you should next check your account settings in Thunderbird. Open "Account settings" > "Server settings" and make sure that the server name, port, user name, and password are correct. You can obtain this information from your email provider.
3. **Check your outgoing mail server (SMTP) settings:** If you are unable to send e-mails, please also check your SMTP settings. Go to "Account settings" > "Outgoing mail server (SMTP)" and check that the settings are correct.
4. **Watch out for server problems:** Occasionally there may be problems with the email server itself that are beyond your control. Check your email provider's website or a website like Down detector to see if other users have reported similar problems.

5. **Temporarily disable antivirus or firewall:** Sometimes antivirus programs or firewalls can block email traffic. Try disabling these programs temporarily to see if this solves the problem. Don't forget to reactivate them afterwards to protect your computer.
6. Contact **your email provider:** If the problem persists after following these steps, please contact your email provider. There may be a problem with your account or your provider's email servers.

9.1.2 THUNDERBIRD CRASHES OR FREEZES

If Thunderbird crashes or freezes frequently, this may indicate various problems. Here are some possible causes and solutions.

1. **Update Thunderbird:** First, you should make sure that you are using the latest version of Thunderbird. Older versions may have known bugs or compatibility issues that have been fixed in newer versions.
2. **Check for add-ons or extensions:** Add-ons or extensions that you have installed can sometimes cause problems. Try starting Thunderbird in safe mode, which disables all add-ons and extensions. If Thunderbird runs smoothly in safe mode, the problem is probably with one of your add-ons or extensions.
3. **Check your Thunderbird profile:** The Thunderbird profile contains all your personal data, including emails, passwords, and add-ons. Sometimes your profile can be corrupted, which can lead to problems. In this case, you can create a new profile to see if the problem persists.
4. **Check for viruses or malware:** Sometimes viruses or other malware can cause programs such as Thunderbird to crash or freeze. Check that your antivirus program is up to date and run a full system scan.
5. **Uninstall and reinstall:** If all other steps fail, you can try uninstalling and reinstalling Thunderbird. Back up your emails and account settings first.

9.1.3 PROBLEMS WITH THE DISPLAY OF E-MAILS

If emails are not displayed correctly in Thunderbird, this can have various causes. Here are some possible solutions:

1. **Check view settings:** Thunderbird allows you to view your emails in different ways. Make sure you have selected the correct one. Go to "***View*** *>* ***"Message Body as"*** and choose between "***Original HTML***", "***Text only,***" or "***Plain text***".

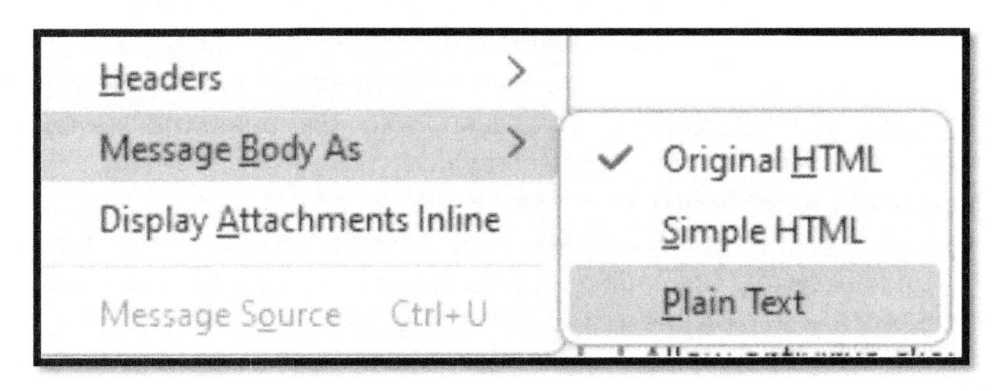

2. **Deactivate add-ons or extensions:** Add-ons or extensions can sometimes affect the display of emails. Start Thunderbird in safe mode to check whether an add-on is causing the problem.
3. **Check your graphics settings:** Your computer's graphics card or graphics driver may, in some cases, affect the display of emails. Update your graphics drivers or change your graphics settings to see if this solves the problem.
4. **Update Thunderbird:** Make sure you are using the latest version of Thunderbird. Older versions may have known bugs or compatibility issues that have been fixed in newer versions.
5. **Contact the sender:** If the problem only occurs with emails from a specific sender, it could be due to the formatting of the email. Contact the sender and ask them to resend the email.

9.1.4 THUNDERBIRD IS SLOW

Slow Thunderbird performance can be caused by a number of issues, including overcrowded inboxes, outdated software, or problems with add-ons. Below you will find some possible solutions:

1. **Update Thunderbird:** Make sure you are using the latest version of Thunderbird. Older versions may have known bugs or compatibility issues that have been fixed in newer versions.
2. **Cleanup the inbox**: An clogged in box can slowdown Thunderbird. can slowdown Thunderbird. Remove old or unnecessary emails and use folders or tags to organize your emails. Also use Thunderbird's automatic archiving function to move older emails.
3. **Compress your folders:** Thunderbird saves your emails in special files called folders. If you delete emails, the information about these emails remains in the folder file until you compress the folder. To do this, right-click on a folder and select "Compress this folder.".
4. **Check your add-ons and extensions:** Every now and then, add-ons or extensions can slowdown Thunderbird. Try starting Thunderbird in safe mode to check whether an add-on is causing the problem.
5. **Check your antivirus settings:** It may happen that some antivirus programs slow down Thunderbird by scanning emails before they are delivered. Please check the settings of your antivirus program and make sure that it does not slow down Thunderbird unnecessarily.
6. **Create a new profile:** If all other steps fail, the problem may be with your Thunderbird profile. Try creating a new profile to see if this improves performance.

See also: 10.7.1 Creating a new profile

9.1.5 PROBLEMS WITH EXTENSIONS

Extensions are a powerful tool to extend the functionality of Thunderbird, but they can also cause problems if they do not work properly. Below are some common problems and solutions:

1. **Faulty extension:** If Thunderbird is having problems after installing a new extension, the extension itself could be the problem. You can try disabling or uninstalling the extension to see if this fixes the problem.

2. **Compatibility issues:** It is not possible for all extensions to be compatible with all versions of Thunderbird. Check that all your extensions are compatible with the version of Thunderbird you are using. You can also try to update Thunderbird or the extension.
3. **Problems with the settings:** The settings of an extension can sometimes cause problems. Test the extension settings and try different options to see if this solves the problem.
4. **Conflicts between extensions:** Occasionally, two or more extensions may conflict with each other and cause problems. Deactivate the extensions one after the other to find out whether a conflict is causing the problem.
5. **Damaged file extensions:** In unfavorable cases, the files of an extension may be corrupted, which can lead to problems. Delete the extension and reinstall it to see if this solves the problem.

9.1.6 THUNDERBIRD DOES NOTDISPLAY NOTIFICATIONS

If Thunderbird does not display any notifications, this can have various causes, from configuration problems to software conflicts. The following solutions are possible:

1. **Check your Thunderbird settings:** Note that Thunderbird has special settings for notifications. Make sure that these are activated. Go to "***Tools" > "Settings" > "General" > "Incoming email messages"*** and make sure that the options for displaying notifications are activated.

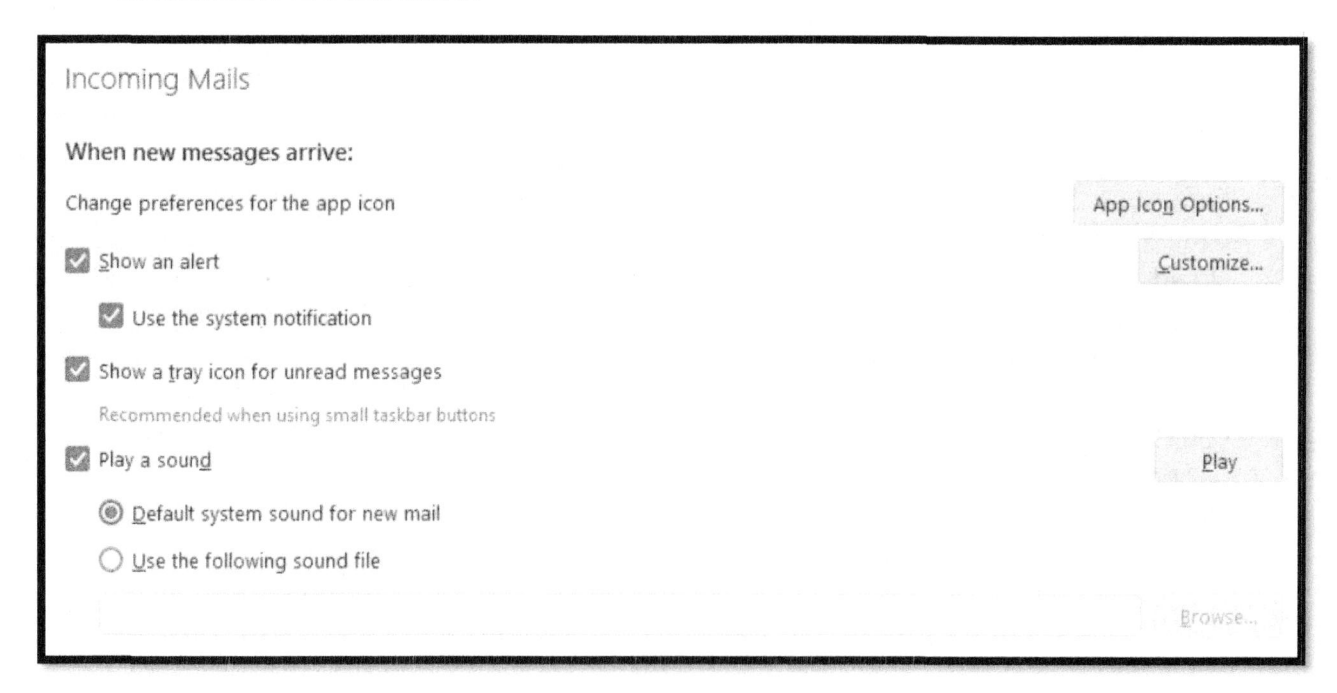

2. **Check your system settings:** The operating system also has settings that control how and when notifications are displayed. Make sure that Thunderbird has the right to display notifications.
3. **Make sure that you are not in "Do Not Disturb" mode:** Most operating systems and Thunderbird have a "Do Not Disturb" mode that mutes all notifications. Make sure that this mode is not activated.

4. **Check your antivirus and firewall settings:** Antivirus programs or firewalls can sometimes prevent notifications from being displayed. Check the settings of these programs to ensure that Thunderbird is not blocked.
5. **Update Thunderbird:** Use the latest version of Thunderbird. Older versions may have known bugs or compatibility issues that have been fixed in newer versions.

9.1.7 THUNDERBIRD CANNOT

CONNECT TO THE SERVER

If Thunderbird cannot connect to the server, there may be various reasons for this, e.g., network problems, incorrect server settings, or problems with your e-mail account. Here are some possibilities:

1. **Check your internet connection:** Make sure that your computer has a stable internet connection. Visit a website in a web browser to see if you are online.
2. **Check the server settings:** In Thunderbird, enter the correct server settings for your email account, including server name, port, and security settings. You can usually obtain this information from your email provider.
3. **Check your e-mail account:** Make sure your email account is working properly. Try logging into your account via a web browser to see if there are any problems.
4. **Check your firewall and antivirus software**: Occasionally, these programs can block communication with the server. You can try disabling them temporarily to see if this fixes the problem.
5. **Update Thunderbird:** It is recommended that you use the latest version of Thunderbird. Earlier versions may have known bugs or compatibility issues that have been fixed in newer versions.
6. **Create a new profile:** If all other steps fail, the problem may be with your Thunderbird profile. You can try creating a new profile to see if this improves the connection.

9.1.8 THUNDERBIRD DOES NOTSAVE PASSWORDS

If your passwords are not saved in Thunderbird, there may be various reasons for this. Here are a few solutions you can try:

1. **Check your settings:** Thunderbird has an option to save passwords. Make sure that this option is activated. You can find this option under "***Settings*** >" ***Privacy & Security***" > "***Passwords.***"

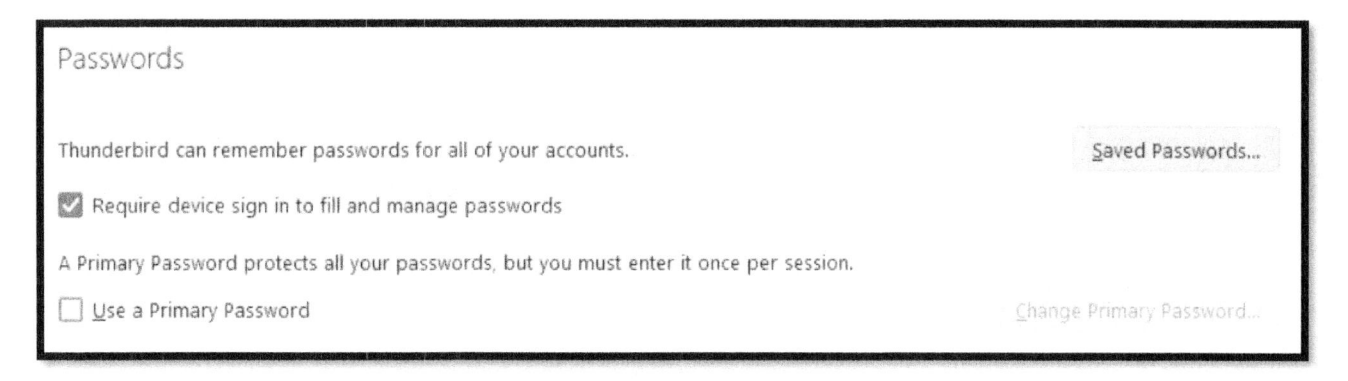

```
Passwords

Thunderbird can remember passwords for all of your accounts.                    Saved Passwords...
☑ Require device sign in to fill and manage passwords

A Primary Password protects all your passwords, but you must enter it once per session.
☐ Use a Primary Password                                                        Change Primary Password...
```

2. **Use a master password:** Master password is an additional password that you must enter in order to access your saved passwords. When using a master password, you must enter it before Thunderbird can use your saved passwords.
3. **Check your profile**: sometimes passwords cannot be saved due to problems with your Thunderbird profile. Create a new profile to see if this solves the problem.
4. **Check your antivirus and firewall settings:** Various security programs can affect the function for saving passwords in Thunderbird. Make sure that the settings of your security software do not affect Thunderbird.

9.1.9 THUNDERBIRD DOES NOTSYNCHRONIZE ALL FOLDERS

There can be various reasons why Thunderbird does not synchronize all folders. Here are some possible solutions:

1. **Check your synchronization settings:** Thunderbird's synchronization settings control which folders are synchronized. You can check and adjust these settings under "***Account settings*" > "*Synchronization & Storage*"**.

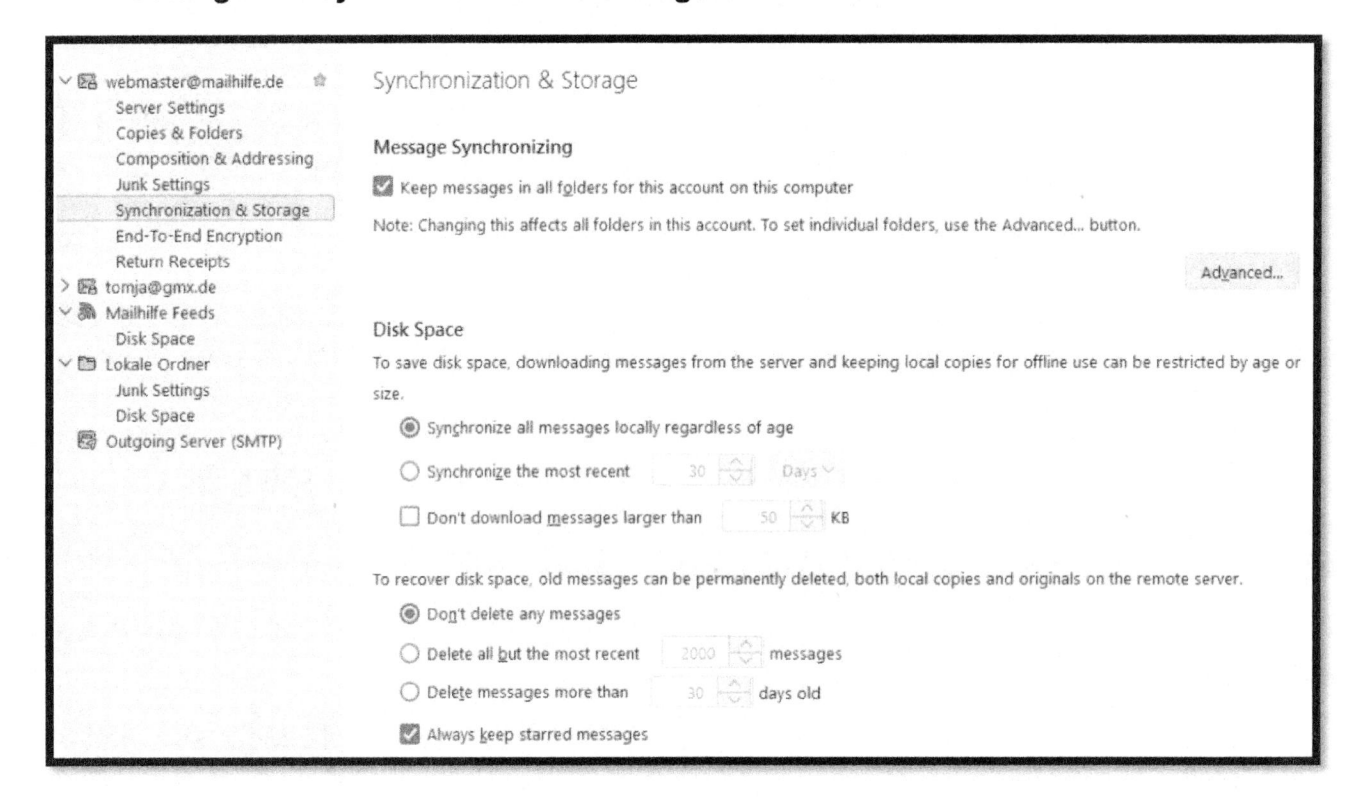

2. **Make sure that the folders are not marked as spam:** Some email providers mark certain folders as spam, which can result in them not being displayed in Thunderbird. Make sure that the missing folders are not marked as spam in the settings of your e-mail account.
3. **Check the IMAP settings of your email provider:** If you are using an IMAP account, make sure that your email provider allows Thunderbird to synchronize all folders. Depending on the provider, there are special settings for this.
4. **Update Thunderbird:** Make sure that you are using the latest version of Thunderbird. Older versions may have known bugs or compatibility issues that have been fixed in newer versions.

9.1.10 THUNDERBIRD CANNOT OPENOR SAVE ATTACHMENTS

If problems occur with Thunderbird when opening or saving attachments, this can have various causes. Here are some suggested solutions:

1. *Check your antivirus software:* Some antivirus programs may prevent you from opening or saving attachments in Thunderbird. Temporarily disable your antivirus program to see if this fixes the problem.
2. *Check your firewall settings:* Sometimes firewalls can prevent file attachments from being downloaded. Make sure that your firewall settings do not affect Thunderbird.
3. *Update Thunderbird:* Make sure you are using the latest version of Thunderbird. Earlier versions may have known bugs or compatibility issues that have been fixed in newer versions.

9.1.1 THUNDERBIRD SENDS DUPLICATE E-MAILS

If Thunderbird sends duplicate e-mails, this can have various causes. Here are some suggested solutions:

1. **Check your outbox:** If your sent emails get stuck in the outbox folder, Thunderbird may try to send them again. Make sure that your sent emails are moved correctly from the outbox folder.
2. **Check your network connection:** An unstable network connection can cause Thunderbird to consider the sending of an email to have failed and try again. Check that you have a stable internet connection when sending emails.
3. **Check the settings of your email account:** Certain email accounts may be configured to move a copy of each email sent to a specific folder. If this folder is configured as the outbox, this may cause Thunderbird to resend the email.
4. **Update Thunderbird:** Use the latest version of Thunderbird. Older versions may contain known bugs or compatibility issues that have been fixed in newer versions.

Duplicate emails can confuse the recipient and look unprofessional. The following steps should help you to resolve the problem and ensure that your emails are sent correctly.

9.2 THUNDERBIRD UPDATES ANDTROUBLESHOOTING

Thunderbird regularly releases updates to close security vulnerabilities, add new features, and fix known issues. Please update Thunderbird regularly to ensure you have the latest security patches and features. Below you will find some tips and information on updating and troubleshooting Thunderbird:

1. **Automatic updates:** In Thunderbird there is a function for automatic updates, which you can activate under *"Settings"* > *"Genera"* > *"Updates"*. This function automatically updates Thunderbird to the latest version as soon as it is available.

> **Updates**
>
> **Thunderbird Updates**
>
> Version 128.2.1esr (64-bit) Release notes   Show Update History
>
> Thunderbird is up to date   Check for Updates
>
> Allow Thunderbird to
>
> ● Automatically install updates (recommended: improved security)
>
> ○ Check for updates, but let me choose whether to install them
>
> ⓘ This setting will apply to all Windows accounts and Thunderbird profiles using this installation of Thunderbird.

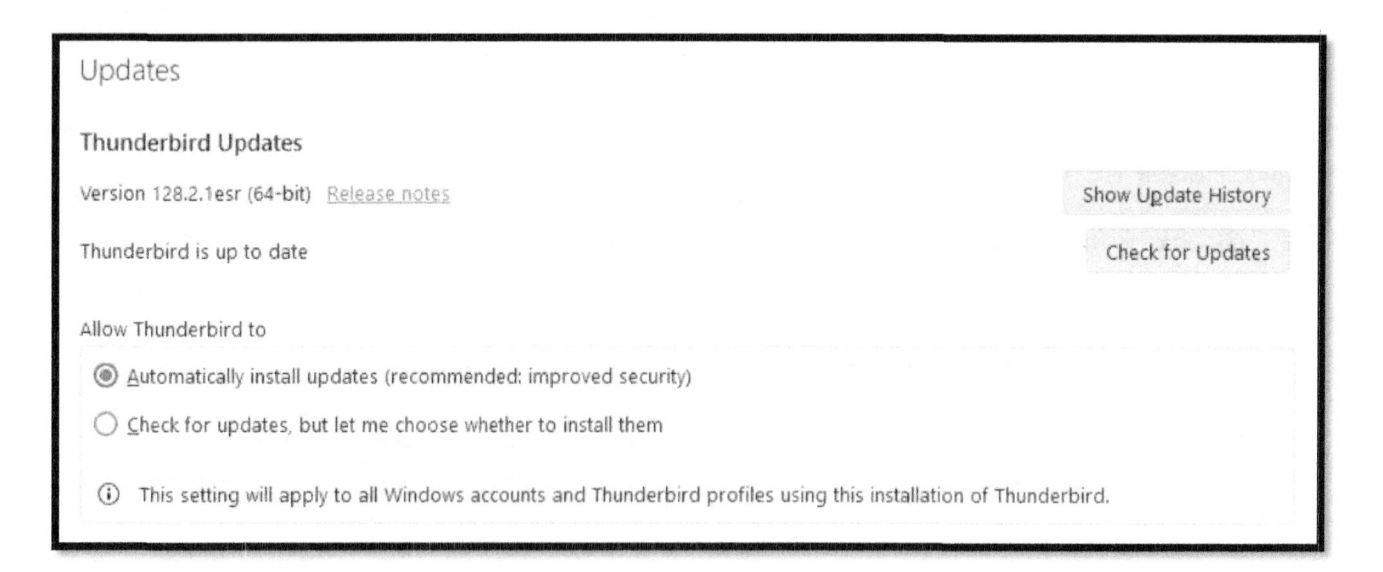

2. **Manual updates:** If you have deactivated automatic updates, you can also update Thunderbird manually. To do this, select **"Help" > "About Thunderbird."** If an update is available, it will be downloaded automatically, and you will be prompted to restart Thunderbird to install the update.

> About Mozilla Thunderbird   ✕
>
> # Thunderbird
>
> 128.2.3esr (64-bit) Release notes
>
> nebula
>
> ✓ *Thunderbird is up to date*
>
> You are currently on the **esr** update channel.
>
> Thunderbird is designed by Mozilla, a global community working together to keep the Web open, public and accessible to all.
>
> Want to help? Make a donation or get involved!
>
> Licensing Information   End-User Rights   Privacy Policy
>
> Mozilla Thunderbird and the Thunderbird logos are trademarks of the Mozilla Foundation.

3. **Troubleshooting after an update:** Occasionally, problems can occur after an update. In such cases, it can be helpful to start Thunderbird in safe mode, which deactivates all extensions and resets some settings to the default values. You can access Safe Mode via "**Help" > "Troubleshooting mode..."**

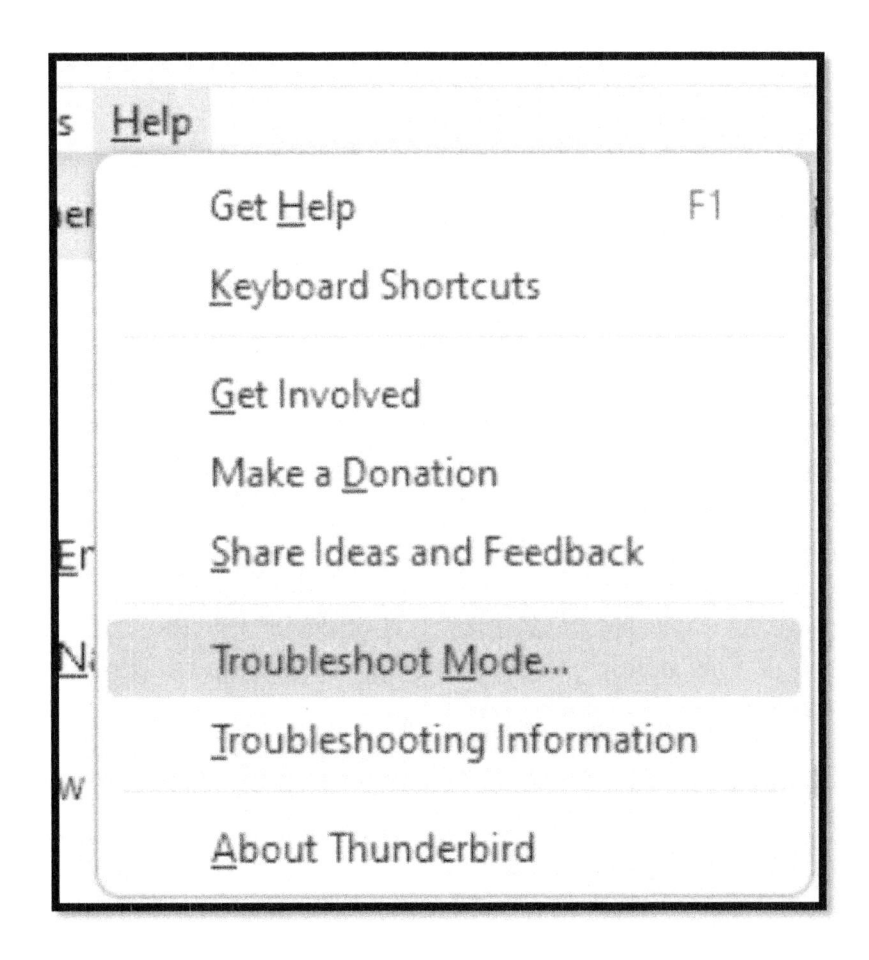

[Screenshot of Thunderbird Help menu showing: Get Help F1, Keyboard Shortcuts, Get Involved, Make a Donation, Share Ideas and Feedback, Troubleshoot Mode... (highlighted), Troubleshooting Information, About Thunderbird]

4. ***Seek support:*** If you still have problems after an update, you can turn to the Thunderbird community. The Thunderbird support forum or Mailhilfe Thunderbird forum is a particularly good place to seek help. Ask your question there and get answers from other Thunderbird users and experts.
5. ***Report a bug:*** If you find a bug in Thunderbird, you can report it to help the developers improve the program. Bugs can be reported via the built-in bug reporting system, which you can find under "***Help***" > "***Send feedback.***".

Through regular updates and proactive troubleshooting, you can ensure that you get the most out of Thunderbird and manage your emails securely and efficiently.

CHAPTER 10: MASTERING ADVANCED SETTINGS

Thunderbird offers a variety of advanced settings that give the user a high degree of control and customization. These settings allow you to customize the behavior and functionality of Thunderbird to your specific needs. In this chapter, we will look at some of these advanced settings and their use in detail.

10.1 CONFIGURATION EDITOR

One of the most powerful tools for customizing Thunderbird is the configuration editor (also known as about:config). This editor gives you access to a wide range of settings that are not normally available via the graphical user interface.

To access the configuration editor, select "*Settings*" from the "*Extras*" menu.

Under "*General*" at the bottom, click on the "*Config Editor*" button.

A warning message will appear informing you that changes to these settings may damage Thunderbird. If you are careful and know what you are doing, you can ignore this warning and continue.

You can change, add, or delete various settings in the configuration editor. Each setting has a name (also called a "key"), a type (such as Boolean, integer, or String) and a value. By changing the value of a setting, you can change the behavior of Thunderbird.

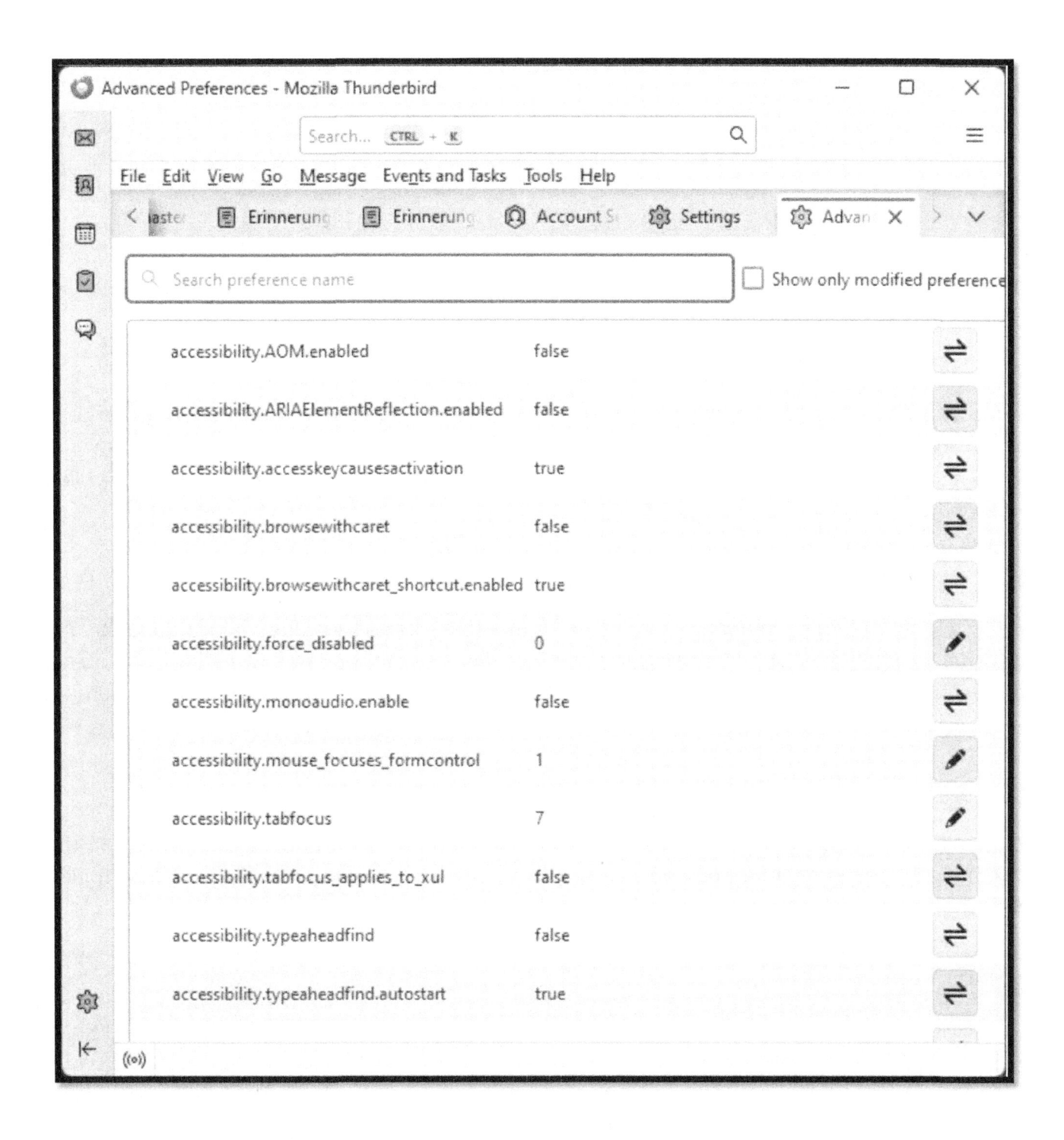

10.2 NETWORK AND STORAGE SETTINGS

In the network and storage settings, you can customize various aspects of Thunderbird's network connection and storage space. For example, you can specify how Thunderbird connects to mail servers, how much storage space Thunderbird should reserve for emails and attachments, and how Thunderbird handles cookies and other web content.

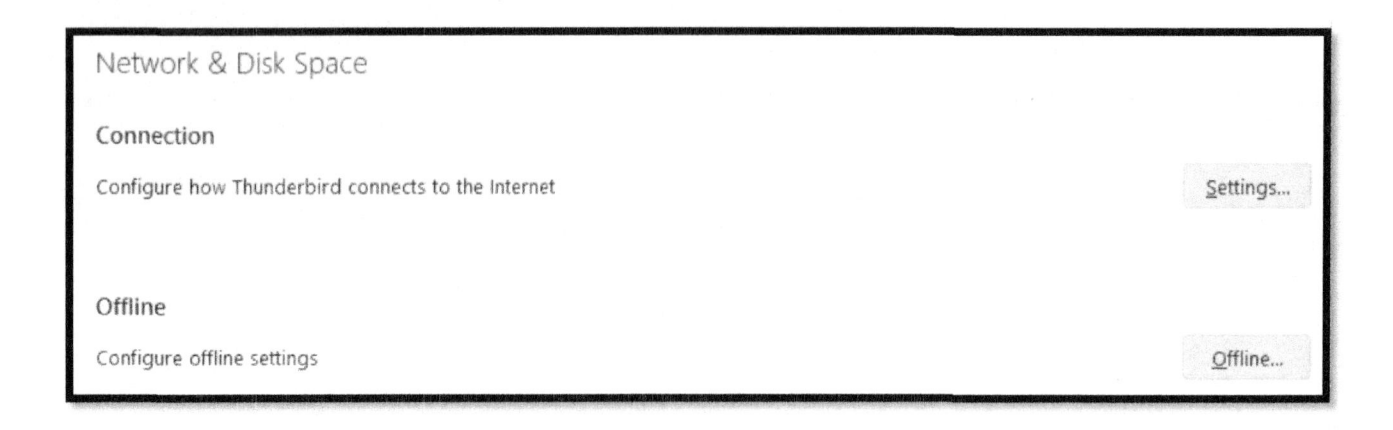

```
Network & Disk Space

Connection
Configure how Thunderbird connects to the Internet                    Settings...


Offline
Configure offline settings                                            Offline...
```

10.3 SECURITY AND PRIVACY SETTINGS

In the security and privacy settings, you can control how Thunderbird handles sensitive data. For example, you can specify whether and when Thunderbird should ask you for passwords, how Thunderbird should deal with spam and what type of data Thunderbird is allowed to collect and report.

10.4 UPDATE SETTINGS

In the update settings, you can control how Thunderbird checks for and installs updates. You can specify whether Thunderbird should automatically check for updates, whether it should ask you before installing an update, and whether it should also check for updates for your add-ons and themes.

10.5 ADD-ON SETTINGS

In the add-on settings, you can control how Thunderbird handles add-ons. Here you can specify whether add-ons should be updated automatically, whether third-party add-ons are permitted, and what type of add-ons Thunderbird is allowed to install.

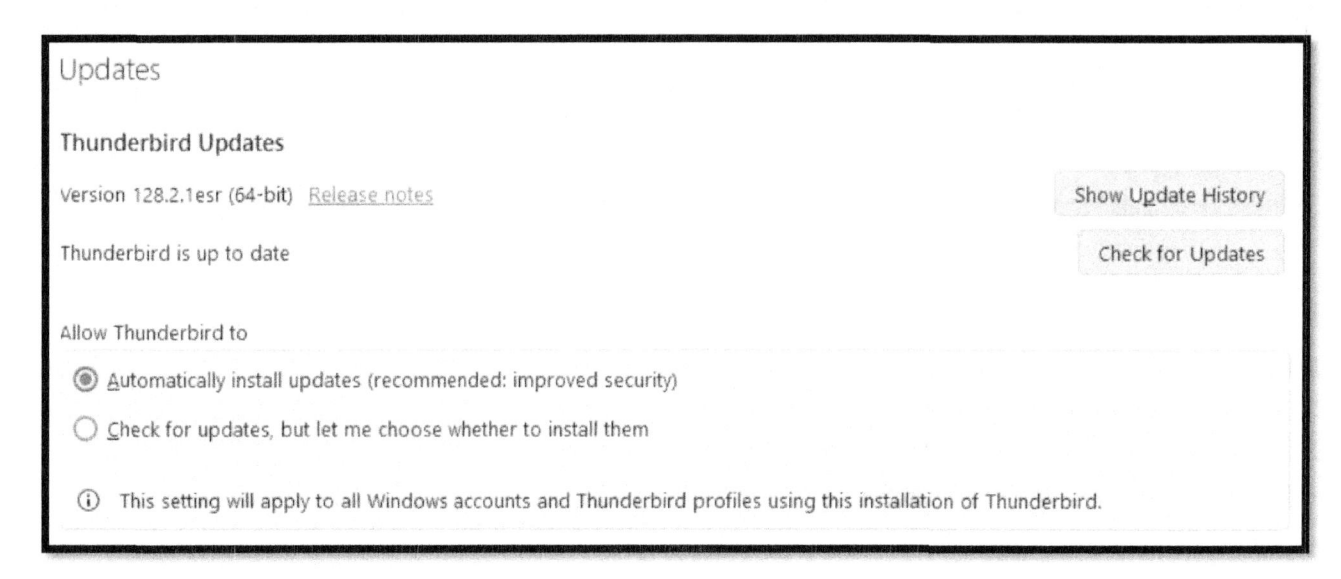

```
Updates

Thunderbird Updates
Version 128.2.1esr (64-bit)  Release notes                 Show Update History

Thunderbird is up to date                                  Check for Updates

Allow Thunderbird to
  ● Automatically install updates (recommended: improved security)
  ○ Check for updates, but let me choose whether to install them

  ⓘ  This setting will apply to all Windows accounts and Thunderbird profiles using this installation of Thunderbird.
```

10.6 ADVANCED MAIL AND NEWS SETTINGS

The advanced mail and news settings allow you to customize various aspects of Thunderbird's mail and news functions. For example, you can define how Thunderbird downloads and saves messages.

10.7 USE OF PROFILES

Thunderbird allows you to create and manage profiles. A profile contains all your personal information, including bookmarks, passwords, extensions, e-mail and newsgroup accounts. By using profiles, multiple users can use Thunderbird on the same computer without mixing their settings and data. You can also create different profiles for different purposes, e.g. one profile for work and another for personal use.

10.7.1 CREATING A NEW PROFILE

To create a new profile in Thunderbird, follow these steps:

1. **Close Thunderbird if it is open.**
2. **Open the Profile Manager.** The way to do this depends on your operating system:
   - Windows: Press the ***Windows key + R to open*** the Run window. Enter "***thunderbird.exe-p***" and press Enter.
   - MacOS: Open the Terminal (located in the Utilities folder). Enter ***/Applications/Thunderbird.app/Contents/MacOS/thunder-bird-bin-profilemanager"*** and press Enter.
   - Linux: Open a terminal window and enter "**thunderbird-profilemanager**" and press Enter.
3. Click on "***Create profile***..." the Profile Manager.

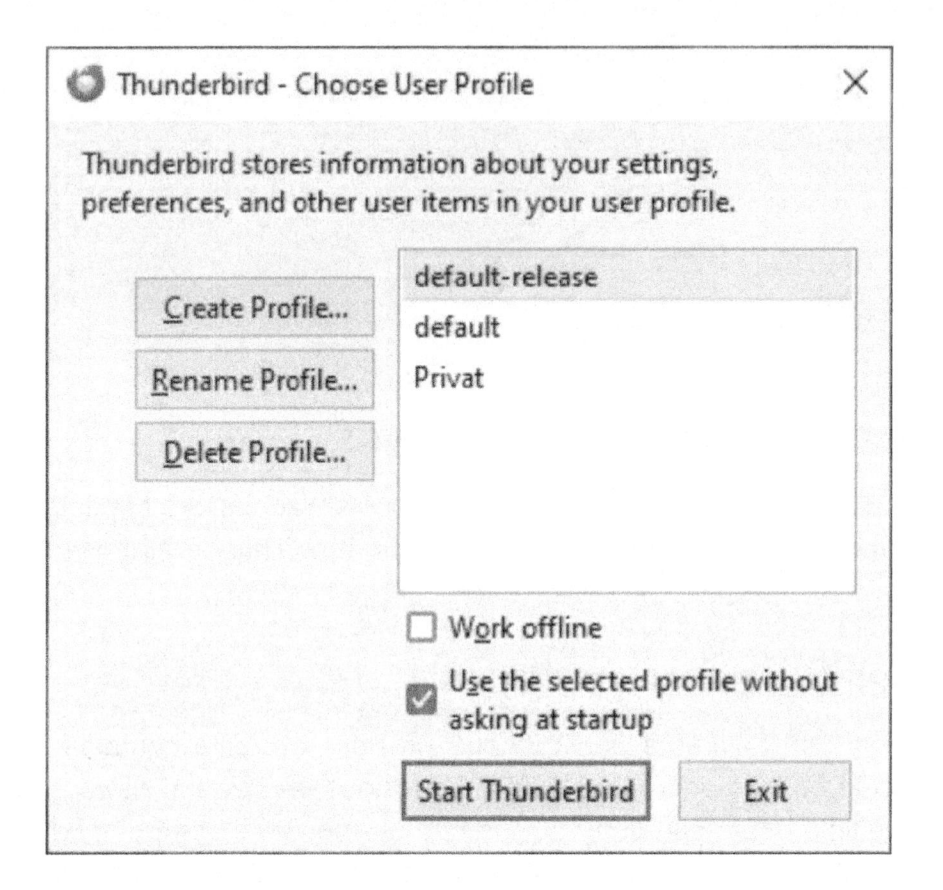

4. Click "**Next**" in the new profile wizard.

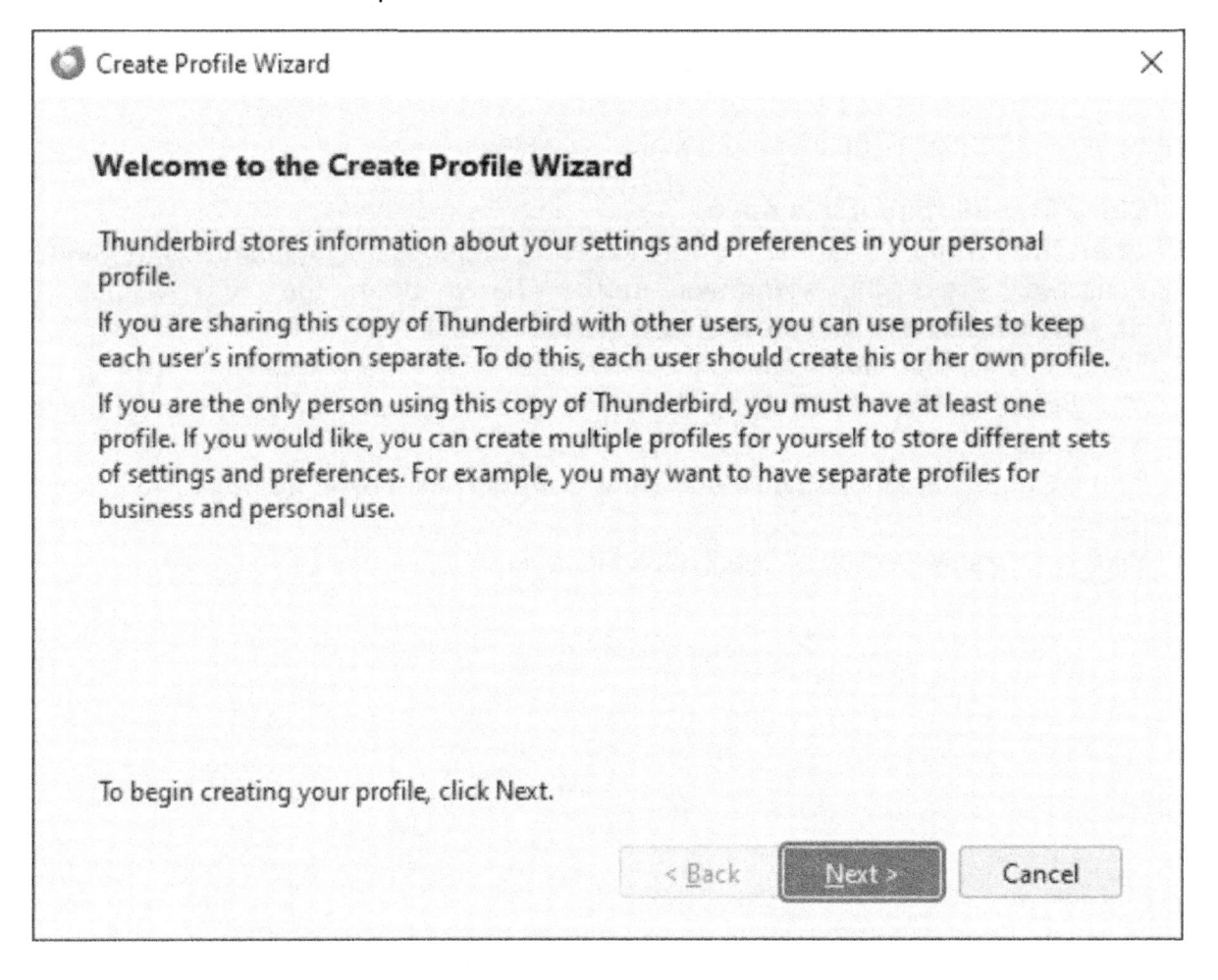

5. Enter a name for the new profile. You can also select a different storage location for the profile, but this is not normally necessary. Click on "**Finish**".

![Create Profile Wizard dialog showing "Completing the Create Profile Wizard" with profile name "Default User" and storage path C:\Users\T\AppData\Roaming\Thunderbird\Profiles\jn99t83n.Default User]

6. Select the newly created profile and click on "**Start Thunderbird.**".

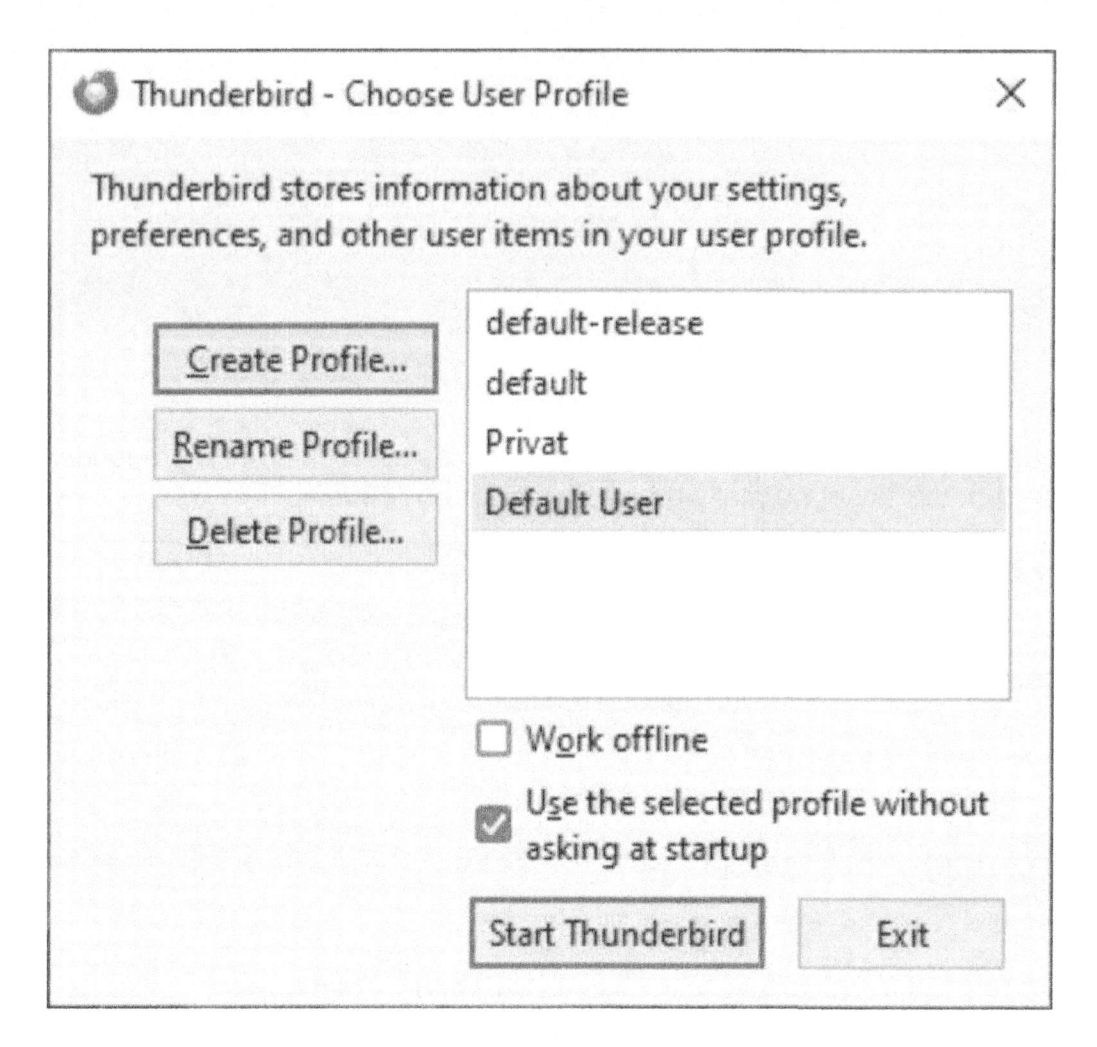

You have now created a new profile in Thunderbird. Each profile has its own e-mails, settings, add-ons, etc. You can switch between pro- files by opening the Profile Manager again and selecting the desired profile. Please note, however, that you must close Thunderbird before you can open the Profile Manager.

10.8 CUSTOMIZING THE USER INTERFACE

Thunderbird offers a variety of options for customizing the user interface. You can change the position and appearance of toolbars and menus, adjust the behavior of tabs and windows, and use various themes and add-ons to change the look of Thunderbird. You can also create and customize keyboard shortcuts to execute frequently used commands faster.

See also 3. personalization and customization

10.9 CUSTOMIZING E-MAIL AND

NEWSGROUP ACCOUNTS

Each email and newsgroup account in Thunderbird has its own settings that you can customize. For example, you can specify how Thunderbird downloads and saves messages from this account, which notifications you receive for new messages, and how Thunderbird handles spam messages in this account. You can also set signatures, address books, and other personal information for each account.

10.10. USING SCRIPTS AND EXTENSIONS

Thunderbird supports the use of scripts and extensions to add additional functionality and customization options. With scripts, you can perform automated tasks such as sorting and filtering messages, sending automated replies, and performing bulk actions. Extensions can add a variety of features, from simple user interface customizations to complex features such as calendar and contacts integration, email encryption, and much more.

A script is essentially a list of commands that are executed by a program. In Thunderbird, these scripts are usually written in JavaScript, as Thunderbird is based on Mozilla's Gecko rendering engine, which uses JavaScript as its primary scripting language.

More on this in chapter 11

10.11. ADJUST DISPLAY SETTINGS

With Thunderbird's display settings, you can customize the appearance of your emails and messages to suit your needs. Change the font and font size, the colors and background, the formatting of quotes, and much more. You can also define how Thunderbird displays HTML messages and which types of content (such as images and videos) should be loaded automatically.

```
Sprache & Erscheinungsbild

Schriftarten und Farben
Standard-Schriftart:  Calibri          ∨    Größe:  17    ∨    Erweitert...
                                                                Farben...
```

10.12. CUSTOMIZE CHAT SETTINGS

If you use Thunderbird's integrated chat functions, you can also customize the chat settings. For example, you can specify which notifications you receive for new messages, how your contact list is displayed, how Thunderbird saves your message history, and much more. You can also set up and manage different chat accounts for different services (such as IRC, XMPP, and Google Talk).

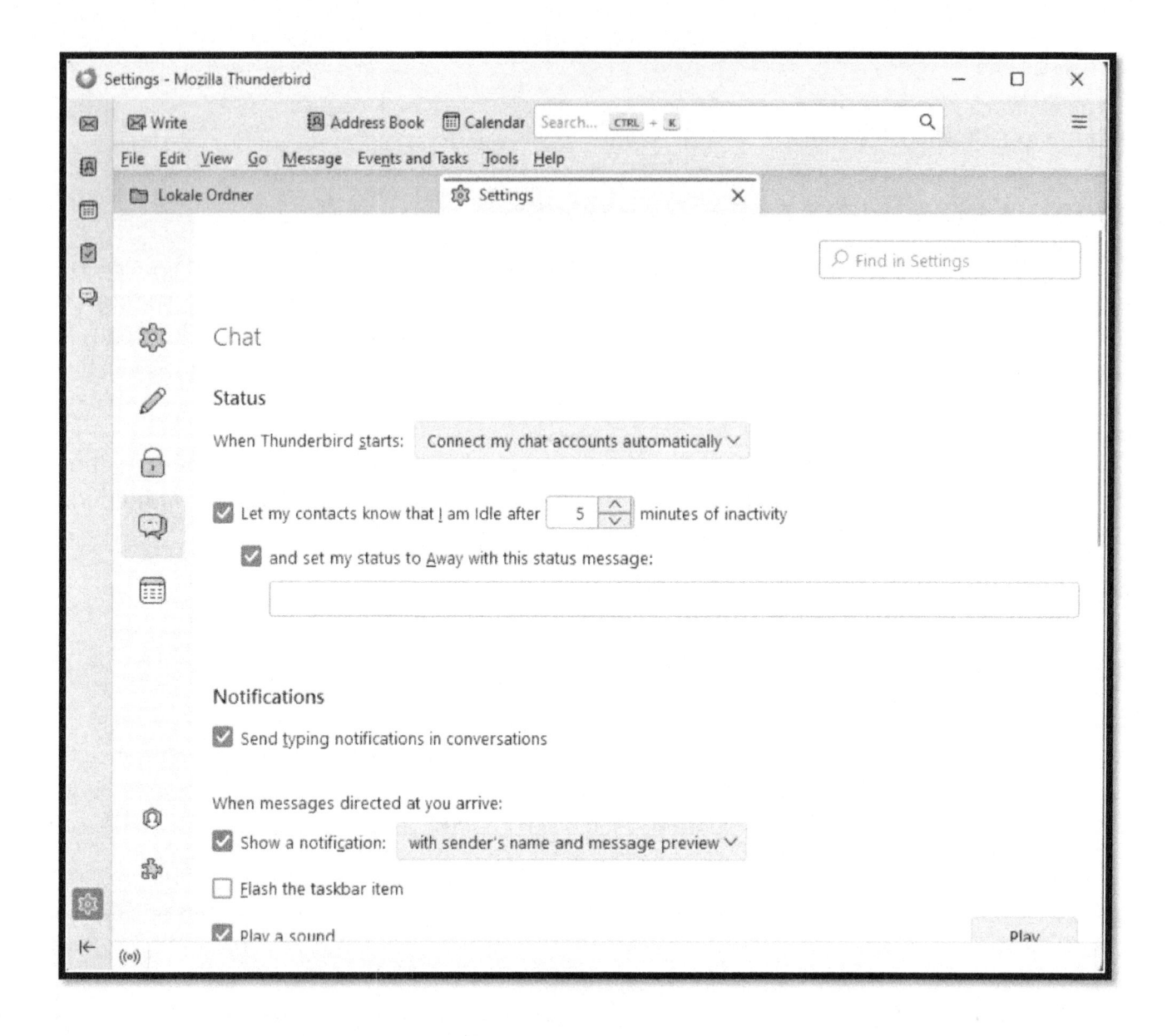

10.13. CUSTOMIZE SECURITY SETTINGS

Thunderbird's security settings allow you to control various aspects of security and privacy. Here you can define how Thunderbird deals with phishing attempts and unsafe content, what types of cookies and other web content Thunderbird accepts, and how Thunderbird stores and protects your personal data and passwords. You can also make settings for the encryption and digital signature of emails.

10.14. CUSTOMIZE DATA PROTECTION SETTINGS

In the privacy settings, you can control which types of data Thunderbird collects and passes on. Whether and how Thunderbird sends usage statistics and crash reports, what data Thunderbird saves in forms and search fields, and how Thunderbird handles cookies and other web content. You can also specify whether and when Thunderbird should ask you for passwords.

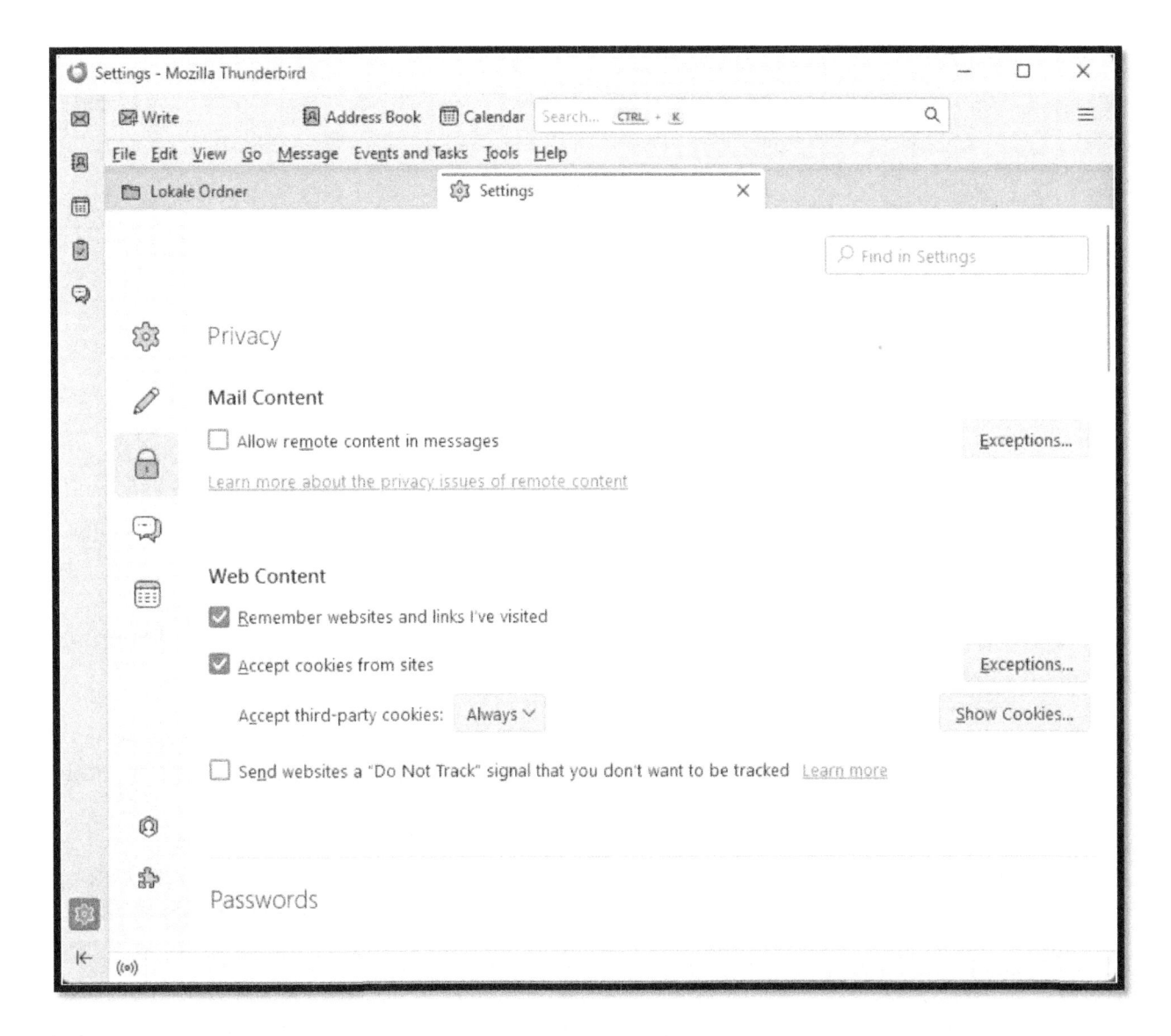

Thanks to these diverse and detailed setting options, Thunderbird offers the user unprecedented control and customization. However, this control and flexibility come with a certain degree of complexity. It is therefore recommended that these settings are changed with caution and understanding.

10.15 THUNDERBIRD START PARAMETERS

Start parameters, also known as command line options, make it possible to perform certain actions when starting Thunderbird or to change the behavior of the software. Here are eight examples of start parameters:

1. **-safe mode:** Starts Thunderbird in safe mode, in which all add-ons are deactivated.
2. **-P <pro filename>:** Starts Thunderbird with a specific profile. Replace <profile name> with the name of the desired profile.
3. **-ProfileManager:** Opens the Profile Manager to create, delete, or change profiles.
4. **-jsconsole:** Opens the JavaScript console.
5. **-mail:** Starts Thunderbird directly in mail mode.
6. **-compose:** Opens a new window for composing an e-mail.
7. **-options:** Opens the dialog box with the settings.

8. **-addressbook:** Opens the address book.

To use these parameters, you must append them to the command used to start Thunderbird. The exact method depends on your operating system:

- **Windows**: Open the Start menu and search for "Thunderbird." Right-click on the Thunderbird icon and select "Properties." In the "Desti-nation" field, you can add the parameters at the end of the line.
- **MacOS**: Open the terminal (located in Applications/Utilities). Enter the path to the Thunderbird application, followed by the desired parameters. For example:' "/Applications/Thunderbird.app/Contents/MacOS/thunderbird-bin" -ProfileManager'.
- **Linux**: Open a terminal window. Enter "thunderbird" followed by the desired parameters, e.g., 'thunderbird

Please note that some of these parameters require you to close Thunderbird completely before you can use them.

CHAPTER 11: CREATING AND USING SCRIPTS

Thunderbird offers the possibility to create user-defined functions and automations using scripts. These scripts can be written in various programming languages, including JavaScript, and then integrated into Thunderbird to automate certain tasks or add additional functions. automate certain tasks or add additional functions.

11.1 BASICS OF SCRIPTING

Creating scripts for Thunderbird requires a basic understanding of programming, especially the language in which the script is to be written. JavaScript is the most commonly used language for Thunderbird scripts, as it is natively supported by the platform.

A script is a series of instructions that are executed by Thunderbird to perform a specific task. These instructions can include sending or receiving emails, changing settings, interacting with the user, or other tasks. include.

To create a script, you need a text editor to write the code and then a way to load and execute the script in Thunderbird.

11.2 SCRIPTING FOR THUNDERBIRD

To create a script for Thunderbird, write the desired code in your text editor and save the file with the extension.js. You can then load the script in Thunderbird via the console.

The precise syntax and structure of your script depends on the programming language and the specific tasks you want to perform. you want to perform. However, there are some general principles that apply to most scripts:

- Every script should have a main function that serves as the entry point for the script. In JavaScript, this function is soften called 'main', but you can give it any name you like.
- Within the main function, you can call other functions, define variables, and implement logic to carry out the desired task.
- You can use external libraries and APIs to add additional functions or simplify complex tasks. simplify complex tasks. In Thunderbird, for example, you can use the Mail API to send and receive emails.

11.3 USING SCRIPTS IN THUNDERBIRD

Once you have created your script, you can use it in Thunderbird. To do this, you must load the script via the console and then call the main function.

To load a script, open the console and navigate to the directory in which your script is stored. Then enter the command 'load("*myscript.js*")', where "*myscript*.js" is the name of your script.

Once the script is loaded, you can execute it by calling the main function. To do this, enter the name of the function followed by square brackets, e.g. ", 'main ()'.

11.4 SCRIPTS FOR THE AUTOMATION OF TASKS

With the help of scripts, recurring tasks can be automated in Thunderbird. For example, you could write a script that automatically moves all emails from a certain sender to a certain folder or a script that automatically sends a reply to certain types of emails.

To create such a script, you would write the code that performs the desired action and then set a condition under which the script is executed. In Thunderbird, you can do this by attaching the script to a filter or a rule that is applied to incoming emails.

11.4.1 EXAMPLE OF AUTOMATING A TASK

To use scripts in Thunderbird, you need an extension such as FiltaQuilla, which enables scripting actions for e-mail filters. is possible. Please note that writing and using scripts requires advanced knowledge and can be potentially dangerous if you do not know exactly what you are doing.

Here is a simple example of a script that automatically moves an email to a specific folder if the subject contains a certain string. This script would be used in an email filter in Thunderbird created with the FiltaQuilla extension.

```javascript
if (subject.contains("order")) {
    moveMessageToFolder("order");
}
```

In this example, the script would check whether the subject of the email contains the string "order." If this is the case, it would call the '*moveMessageToFolder*' function to move the email to the "Orders" folder.

Note that this is a very simple example and that real scripts can be much more complex. For example, they could contain multiple conditions and actions, retrieve data from external sources, perform complex calculations, and much more.

11.5 SCRIPTS FOR CUSTOMIZINGTHUNDERBIRD

Apart from the automation of tasks, scripts can also be used to customize the functionality and appearance of Thunderbird. For example, you can write a script that adds additional menu options, changes the behavior of keyboard shortcuts, or changes the appearance of the Thunderbird interface.

To do this, write the code that makes the desired changes and configure the script so that it is loaded when Thunderbird is started. In Thunderbird, you can do this by adding the script to the "userChrome.js" or "userContent.js" folder in your Thunderbird profile directory.

11.6 SAFETY AND TROUBLESHOOTING

Although scripts are a powerful tool for customizing and automating Thunderbird, it is important to exercise caution when using them. Poorly written or malicious scripts can affect the functionality of Thunderbird or put your data and privacy at risk.

Only use scripts that you have written yourself or that come from a trustworthy source. Always check the code of a script before you use it to ensure that it does not carry out any malicious actions.

If you have problems with a script, you can run it in the console for troubleshooting. The console will display error messages and debugging information that can help you identify and fix the problem. It is also a good idea to make regular backups of your scripts and Thunderbird data to avoid data loss.

With this information, you should be able to create and use scripts for Thunderbird to increase your productivity and customize Thunderbird to your specific needs.

11.7 SCRIPTS FOR MANAGING EXTENSIONS

Scripts can also be used to automate the management of Thunderbird extensions. For example, a script could be written to automatically install or remove certain extensions, or to change the settings of extensions.

To do this, you would write the code that performs the desired action and then configure the script to run on demand. In Thunderbird, you can do this by adding the script to the "extensions" folder in your Thunderbird profile directory.

11.8 SCRIPTS FOR INTEGRATION

WITH OTHER APPLICATIONS

You can use scripts to integrate Thunderbird with other applications on your computer. For example, you could write a script that retrieves information from a database or another program and displays it in Thunderbird, or a script that triggers an action in Thunderbird when a certain condition is met in another application.

You create such a script by writing the code that performs the desired integration and then configuring the script to run on demand. In the case of Thunderbird, you can do this by adding the script to the "*integrations*" folder in your Thunderbird profile directory.

11.9 SCRIPTS FOR USER-DEFINED FUNCTIONS

Finally, scripts can be used to create completely new functions in Thunderbird. For example, you could write a script that creates a new type of email filter, a script that provides additional statistics about your email usage, or a script that creates a completely new user interface for Thunderbird.

Programming such scripts requires a deeper understanding of programming and possibly also of Thunderbird's code base, but the possibilities are almost unlimited. With enough creativity and technical know-how, Thunderbird can be made into almost any desired form.

11.10 CONCLUSION

Developing and using scripts in Thunderbird is a powerful way to extend the functionality of the program and adapt it to your specific needs. Regardless of whether you want to automate recurring tasks automate repetitive tasks, customize the user interface, integrate the program with other applications or create completely new features, scripts can help you do it. With a basic knowledge of programming and a willingness to experiment, you can take full advantage of this feature.

CONCLUSION

In the journey of mastering any tool, there comes a point when the user no longer simply operates it; they become fully immersed, wielding it with ease and intention. This transformation is the essence of truly understanding a powerful application, such as Thunderbird. From the first moments of installation and setup to fully embracing the advanced features and customizing the interface to match individual needs, the journey through Thunderbird has likely shown you how versatile, flexible, and empowering a dedicated email client can be.

For many users, Thunderbird is more than an application; it's a gateway to a smoother, more productive digital life. It's where you manage communications, maintain relationships, organize tasks, and even safeguard sensitive information. This email client, while simple on the surface, has demonstrated that it is capable of delivering a robust suite of features tailored to the needs of both beginners and power users alike. And through this guide, you've unlocked the potential to manage not only your emails but also your time, contacts, and tasks in a way that's efficient and meaningful to you.

As you've seen, Thunderbird's strength lies not only in its foundational email capabilities but in its ability to integrate seamlessly with every aspect of digital communication. The robust setup process provides a stable platform, while the personalization features let you shape Thunderbird to reflect your style and optimize your workflow. From choosing themes to setting up shortcuts, Thunderbird's flexibility makes it a uniquely personal tool in a field where one-size-fits-all solutions are common. This personalization is more than just an aesthetic choice—it's a reflection of your unique needs and working style, allowing Thunderbird to serve you as a productivity tool crafted precisely for you.

Beyond its foundational capabilities, Thunderbird introduces you to a world where email management is no longer a chore but an empowered process. Learning to effectively organize and filter emails, mastering the search functions, and implementing the tagging and categorizing features has shown how quickly an inbox that feels unmanageable can be transformed into a neatly organized communication hub. The skills you've gained in managing your email with Thunderbird can extend to other areas of digital life, building the foundation for habits that keep you organized, focused, and productive.

The calendar and task management features that Thunderbird offers provide a natural complement to its email functionality. Where emails serve as the record of communications and responsibilities, the calendar and task tools give you the means to plan, schedule, and prioritize. If you've taken full advantage of these features, then by now, Thunderbird is likely more than just your email client; it's your personal organizer, keeping track of appointments, deadlines, and events without the need for external applications. Integrating your emails, contacts, and calendar into one streamlined workflow makes it easier to stay on top of commitments, and it turns Thunderbird into an all-encompassing digital assistant.

The contact management capabilities that Thunderbird offers also play a vital role in its utility. In a world where communication and networking are pivotal, having an organized address book can make all the difference. The address book is more than just a list of names and email addresses—it's a powerful tool that enables you to manage relationships, remember important details, and make your interactions more effective and personal. Thunderbird's address book lets you effortlessly store, organize, and retrieve contact information, whether for personal connections or business purposes. This integration between email, tasks, and contacts allows Thunderbird to simplify and centralize your communication needs.

One of Thunderbird's most valuable attributes is its commitment to security and privacy. As digital threats evolve, the importance of secure communication has never been more critical. In exploring Thunderbird's security features, from spam filters to end-to-end encryption options, you've gained tools that empower you to protect your data and your communications. This security-conscious approach is especially vital for anyone handling sensitive information, and Thunderbird's options for encryption and privacy settings allow you to interact confidently in a digital world where security concerns are pervasive. The built-in tools to protect you from spam, phishing, and other threats not only safeguard your information but also bring peace of mind, ensuring that your email experience is both productive and secure.

While Thunderbird is designed to be user-friendly, you may have encountered challenges along the way—troubleshooting issues, adjusting configurations, or experimenting with new features. Thunderbird's supportive community and extensive documentation are an invaluable resource here, demonstrating the power of open-source software and its user-driven development approach. Any software has a learning curve, and it's through these challenges that you often discover Thunderbird's deeper capabilities. With a wide array of resources and a helpful user community, Thunderbird makes overcoming hurdles not only possible but empowering, adding another layer of resilience to your digital toolkit.

For those who have delved into Thunderbird's advanced settings and scripting capabilities, the experience has likely been one of exploration and discovery. These advanced tools are designed for users who want to take their experience to the next level, automating repetitive tasks and customizing Thunderbird to suit complex workflows. If you've explored scripting, you've unlocked a new level of efficiency, turning Thunderbird into more than just an application—it becomes a customized productivity engine. By automating responses, creating specific filters, and using scripts to streamline workflows, Thunderbird adapts to your unique needs, transforming the way you interact with email and tasks.

Reflecting on your journey with Thunderbird, it becomes clear that the process of learning this tool mirrors the process of mastering any skill. There were foundational steps, challenges to overcome, and moments of realization as you unlocked new capabilities. As you've progressed, Thunderbird has evolved from a simple tool to a sophisticated, multifaceted resource that empowers you to manage communications, stay organized, and work with confidence and security.

The skills and strategies you've gained through using Thunderbird extend beyond the application itself. You've developed habits of organization, prioritization, and digital security that can serve you in a variety of contexts. Whether managing email for business, keeping personal communications organized, or simply optimizing your digital life, these habits are transferable and will continue to benefit you regardless of the tools you use in the future. Thunderbird is unique in its ability to teach such a comprehensive approach to digital management, embedding these valuable skills into your daily routine.

Your relationship with Thunderbird doesn't end with the completion of this guide. Thunderbird, like all good software, continues to grow and evolve, with new updates, features, and improvements driven by a community that's as invested in its future as you are in your productivity. Staying engaged with Thunderbird's updates and new add-ons ensures you'll continue to find new ways to enhance your experience. As Mozilla and the open-source community release enhancements, you'll be able to stay at the forefront of email technology and productivity, benefitting from the latest advancements in digital communication.

As you close this guide, it's clear that Thunderbird is far more than an email client. It's a testament to the power of open-source software and the idea that technology should serve the user's needs, not dictate them. Thunderbird's ethos is rooted in empowerment, flexibility, and user-centric development. Choosing Thunderbird means choosing to be in control of your digital communication, and in a world where that control is often lacking, Thunderbird's dedication to customization and security is a welcome change.

This guide has aimed to equip you with both the practical skills and the deeper understanding needed to make the most of Thunderbird. From basic navigation to advanced automation, every section has been designed to give you confidence in using this tool, regardless of your starting point. Whether you began as a novice or were already familiar with email clients, Thunderbird offers something for every level, meeting each user where they are and growing alongside them.

The skills you've developed will enable you to be more efficient, more secure, and more connected in both personal and professional contexts. Thunderbird, as a tool, complements your growth by providing the infrastructure and flexibility to handle whatever your email and communication needs may be. You've learned not just to manage your inbox but to master it, transforming email from a task into a streamlined part of your productivity ecosystem.

Finally, remember that Thunderbird is a living, evolving project. By using it and contributing feedback to its community, you play a role in its continued development. Open-source software thrives on its users' experiences, and each piece of feedback, every bug report, and each suggestion contributes to making Thunderbird even better. Your journey with Thunderbird is part of a larger story, one in which users and developers collaborate to build a tool that serves everyone. As you continue to explore and engage with Thunderbird, you become an active participant in its mission—a mission to make email management secure, accessible, and empowering.

As you move forward, may Thunderbird continue to be a reliable partner in all your digital communication endeavors. This tool is more than capable of adapting to your needs, helping you stay organized, connected, and in control of your digital world. Embrace the freedom, flexibility, and empowerment Thunderbird provides, and let it guide you to new heights of productivity and confidence in managing your communication.

Thank you for taking this journey with Thunderbird, and may your experience be as rewarding and transformative as the software itself. Here's to countless organized inboxes, secured communications, and a digital life managed with grace and efficiency. You're now equipped not only to use Thunderbird but to master it fully, making it an integral part of your digital journey.

Printed in Great Britain
by Amazon